Soaring Across Country

Also by Bill Scull

PRINCIPLES OF FLIGHT (*B. G. A.*)

Soaring
Across Country

Bill Scull F.R.Ae.S.

Director of Operations British Gliding Association

PELHAM BOOKS
London

First published in Britain by
Pelham Books Ltd
27 Wrights Lane
Kensington, London W8
1979
Reprinted 1986

© 1979 W. G. Scull

All Rights Reserved. No part of this publication may be reproduced, stored in
a retrieval system, or transmitted, in any form or by any means, electronic,
mechanical, photocopying, recording or otherwise, without the prior
permission of the Copyright owner.

ISBN 0 7207 1153 3

Photoset in Great Britain by D. P. Media Ltd
Printed in Great Britain by
Hollen Street Press Ltd at Slough
and bound by Butler and Tanner, Frome

Contents

Illustrations

Line Drawings

Photographs

Introduction

This book sets out to do something that has never, to the best of my knowledge, been tried before: to guide you from your early solo flights to the time when you may regard yourself as an 'established' soaring pilot, and start to get more fulfilment from the sport.

I believe that a glider pilot's aspirations are limited for the simple reason that he cannot conceive of ever achieving the next goal; as a pilot under training, going solo may have seemed unattainable but once solo, there are so many things to attempt. The first is soaring – gliding without soaring is a pastime lacking in stimulation or much purpose. Even soaring should have a particular aim, because staying aloft is scarcely an end in itself.

Progress towards becoming a *soaring* pilot, as opposed to a *gliding* one, is often slow. Help from instructors is limited, or simply not available, because their preoccupation is with basic training. There are, of course, exceptions; at some clubs a student is confident at soaring by the time he goes solo – or soon after. Some examples will serve to illustrate the point. A solo pilot still being checked each day was flying with his Chief Flying Instructor (CFI); when given permission to fly solo, he asked if he was allowed to soar. The CFI said 'Yes' so this student on his eighth solo flight stayed up for more than five hours to qualify for the Silver 'C' duration. Another pilot attending an Instructors' Course was apologetic because he hadn't completed the requisite 35 hours' experience in command; he had however made two cross-country flights, the first for Silver 'C' distance (50 km) and the second a flight of over 300 kilometres for the Gold 'C' distance. The exceptional pilot will have a hundred hours before completing this task, and the average will have nearer two hundred.

Examples like this, though, really are the exception, and it is not with the pilot who is eventually going to get his Gold 'C' that I am concerned – although even he could find this book of benefit. The pilots who need the help are those who may never experience the true thrill of soaring because they will never fly across country. In almost the same category are those pilots who complete their Silver 'C' and then do not fly away again. Pilots in either category could go far, literally, with a little help.

The nature of the help required varies; with an increasing awareness amongst instructors of the need for advanced training, three methods have evolved. First the dual cross-country flight to which there are many obstacles: readily available two-seaters of good performance, a lack of instructors with enough recent experience and a widespread reluctance to let the club two-seater go away. Second is the escorted cross-country; here an experienced cross-country pilot – usually an instructor as well – will take a group of pilots, each flying gliders of similar performance, and escort them, helping them to find lift and in any other way possible. The third way is to do with creating the right environment; bringing pilots together with the express purpose of flying cross-country in a task week, when each day a specific task is set, for example (certainly something less intimidating than a competition is desirable).

The task-week concept is by no means original. If well organised it will foster the right spirit – encouraging the participant to improve his performance little by little. Whether the pilot completes the task is immaterial; he gains confidence as a result of improved skill in soaring, navigation and, probably, making field landings. Whether he knew it or not, it was confidence that was lacking in the first place.

You may wonder why this book is necessary if there are these alternative ways of helping pilots to improve their cross-country skills. The reason is that facilities are limited, and the majority of pilots are left to fend for themselves. With a little help from a sympathetic instructor, and a basic plan to make maximum use of your airborne time, then you can progress steadily towards your first cross-country flight. If you have already flown cross-country, then this should help you to go farther and faster.

The first need, however, is guidance in any solo flying, to give it a sense of purpose; you can do much in flying locally – around your home airfield, that is – which will help develop the skills necessary to become a moderately competent and confident cross-country pilot.

In the final analysis of course, it is motivation that counts, and this is something which it is impossible to implant or instil except perhaps from the instructor's own enthusiasm. However, there may be little active encouragement to progress, which may make the pilot feel unduly restricted. While it is essential to gain a certain amount of experience before taking the next step – be it the first field landing or first cross-country – in the interests of safety, this gaining of experience may seem little more than accumulating of hours and launches in a log book.

The problem of giving instruction (or getting it) which will allow a steady development of a pilot's skill in all aspects of soaring and the confidence that goes with it, is what this book is all about.

Finally, it should be recognised there are many complex factors which influence a pilot's progress. The obvious ones of confidence and psychological problems apart, motivation and environmental factors are significant. I hope I have recognised all these in this attempt to help you get more fulfilment from your gliding.

Acknowledgements

I am indebted to Alan Purnell for some of the barograph traces, Paul Thompson for 'Why Fly MacCready?' and to John Williamson for permission to use his glide calculator as well as commenting constructively on the manuscript; also to Vic Carr, the Chairman of the British Gliding Association's Instructor Committee, who was a source of enthusiasm, and also checked the manuscript – as did others too numerous to mention individually.

In particular I would like to thank my wife, Yvonne, who has been a source of strength throughout my years of gliding; who has never complained when gliding took more than its fair share of my time, and has cheerfully entertained countless gliding friends and acquaintances.

Photo Credits

A sample cross-country: David Ballard (2, 4, 5, 8, 10, 11, 12, 13, 14, 15, 16, 17, 18, 19, 20, 21); all other pictures taken by the author.

1 Flying Accuracy

It may be surprising to start a book on cross-country flying with a chapter on flying accuracy, but for most pilots there is considerable room for improvement in that respect. No pilot can assess objectively the accuracy with which he flies, it is only in retrospect – from a standpoint of some experience – that he can look back and recognise how poor a pilot he was years ago. Even this critical assessment of one's ability cannot be made if, in fact, one has not been progressively extended and done more hours of flying in each successive year. The marginally competent pilot probably flies, on average, ten hours a year; by the time he has a hundred hours in his log book he regards himself as 'experienced'. He can cope with taking off and landing and with some local soaring, but if he has to deal with an awkward-height aerotow rope break then his lack of ability will be evident.

It is difficult to convince a pilot that he is lacking in skill. If an instructor shows the pilot how much better a particular manoeuvre can be done, the pilot will say, 'Well you're an instructor – I'd expect you to be able to do it better', or 'I never do very well when I'm being checked'. Such remarks are valid, up to a point, but if the pilot cannot be convinced that there is scope for improvement, then the chances of improving piloting skills are slim.

Equally a cold-blooded, critical, detailed analysis of a check flight has the risk that a pilot will misunderstand the real motivation behind it, which is to make him take real pride in what he is doing and not settle for second-best. This is something that a good instructor will try and instil into his students from the very outset of training by gradually exacting a higher and higher standard. This message or emphasis is lessened because the majority of students fly with a number of instructors in the course of basic training, and the student pilot may only be concerned with the minimum standard. If, by first-solo stage, or the time he is remote from daily flying checks, this philosophy of accuracy has not been instilled, then the only hope is that the pilot will discover it for himself.

What can be done then for your flying skill if you want to become a better pilot? The answer lies, first of all, in developing a critical attitude towards all phases of flight. The need – and this will become more evident later – is to become much more accurate, so that with improved skill much less of one's concentration is needed on handling the glider, allowing more attention to airmanship, soaring and navigation; the cross-country skills. So the improvement of one's flying skills requires a detailed analysis of various phases of flight and the development of a critical faculty and, underlying this, a philosophy that to 'do it right' is the only way. In talking to other pilots who already have this philosophy, it is easy to establish the common aim – but then, 'preaching to the converted' was never difficult. Two examples will serve to illustrate this point. An airline captain being checked on the flight simulator was making an approach; the speed should have been 119 kt for the particular phase of approach. The training captain supervising made critical comment because it was 120 kt. That's the standard to aim at.

On a more personal note, it is always my aim in landing an aeroplane on a runway to have the nosewheel (in a tricycle undercarriage aircraft) touch down exactly on the runway centre-line and moreover to touch down on a particular point along the line. The fundamental point – it's really not that difficult if you set your mind to it – is that such discipline is essential to developing skill. If it helps you survive a critical-height launch failure or other potential emergency, then the practice and discipline will have been worthwhile.

Before looking at the various phases of flight in which you should seek to improve your skills, there are some significant influences which may stem from the way in which you were trained.

Basic flying training
In learning to glide, the actual circumstances are much more critical than many students appreciate. While in retrospect it may appear that the student could select, and go to, the club offering the best means of training, that is rarely the case. Anyone interested simply goes along to his nearest gliding club and accepts what they offer.

This will vary from the simplest winch- or autotow-launch schemes to all-aerotow, with perhaps the use of motor gliders, or, of course, a mixture. Supporters of any one particular means of training will no doubt argue that their method is best; certainly, whatever the method of launching, it is possible to produce a pilot. What should be of real concern however, are the limitations imposed by the system. The 'pros and cons' of each should be recognised if one is to set about overcoming the inherent handicaps.

Winch or autotow only
The initial problem with this is the lack of time in the air to develop a really good handling skill; matters are made worse by instructors who, although motivated to give 'value for money' – a laudable aim – push their students into attempting things rather too soon, that is before they can fly the glider properly.

The eventual end-product is a pilot who is very good at doing launches, flying circuits and at landing, but good at little else. The opportunity to soar may well have been limited due to a lack of launch height and time in the air to search for thermals, so the pilot has to teach himself to soar. That is often a long and frustrating business.

Such a pilot needs to move to a different club or site to improve his chances of soaring, where either the terrain is better or the chance of contacting lift is improved because the launches are by aerotow; some soaring training would also be beneficial.

Aerotow
Aerotow training gives an adequate amount of time in the air from the outset in which to develop the basic handling skills. In this respect, it offers an almost ideal training method. Given suitable .weather, a pilot will be able to soar, and by the time he goes solo should be capable of soaring flights using more than one thermal; that is, he is competent not only to soar, but also to select the next likely source of lift.

The only possible problem for a pilot trained in an aerotow-only club concerns landings; he may never or rarely have made a bad one, and so may not quite know what to do when one goes wrong. It may help if instructors contrive errors in the landing phase to see that the student reacts correctly. It will be too late if any shortcomings are discovered on solo flights.

Motor gliders

This training method is an expeditious one for the person with little time to spare. The delusion that gliding requires anything less than total commitment still does not last long, though, because after four or five hours on the motor glider the student moves to conventional gliding and finds out how frustrating it can be. Meanwhile, during his motor glider training, he has learnt little or nothing of gliding operations and airmanship, a lack which can only be detrimental. Exposure to a gliding environment is the principal means of pilot education. Despite this deficiency, motor-glider training can get a pilot off to a good start provided its limitations are borne in mind by instructors. Good co-ordination and a high standard of general handling can be achieved because the time-in-the-air requirement can be fulfilled even more conveniently than in aerotow training.

These alternative ways in which one can start gliding should be borne in mind, as they influence the degree of emphasis on various points in the rest of this chapter.

Basic Handling

Turning

First of all the problems. In learning to fly, a student is first shown and then tries the effect of controls; he is then shown how to turn. Turning is really quite a complex manoeuvre, requiring co-ordinated use of all three controls. A student, given a model to copy, then makes his subsequent attempts with assistance, sometimes directly on the controls, but more usually by prompts. Typical faults during early attempts at this exercise are failure to use the elevator to stop the nose from dropping, and misuse of the rudder. Unless the student is constrained at this stage to turn correctly, by being given sufficient help, he can easily develop habits, such as over-ruddering the turn entry, which are likely to stay with him for a very long time, perhaps always. The reason for this is not all that profound; habits of any sort are easy to acquire and very difficult to shed. Even when one has learnt to make good turns, initial bad habits may re-appear at moments of stress. It may seem relevant only to instructors, but if in acquiring the basic skills students can make the minimum of mistakes, they have a better chance of becoming accurate pilots.

However, you, reader, are almost certainly an established pilot with cross-country aspirations; what can be done to improve your skills and remedy, if necessary, the neglect of past months or years? First of all, the next time you go flying, attempt some turns steeper than has been your habit in the past. The actual angle of bank is not too critical to start with – just steeper than usual. Before it is possible to become specific on bank angle, some means of quantifying that angle must be found. The reason for this is that the majority of pilots over-estimate bank angle. Turns usually have much less bank than the pilot thinks. One way of checking the angle is by timed turns at given speeds; at a speed of 45 knots, a turn with 45° of bank will take approximately 15 seconds, whilst the same bank at a speed of 60 knots will take almost 20 seconds. So an immediate and simple way to check your impressions of bank angle is the timed turn. You might find that until you have practised a little it is difficult to maintain a constant speed, and obviously conditions such as turbulent or thermic air will influence this.

Other factors, however, are relevant, which may be due to long-established habits such as turning with only small angles of bank. In the course of many such turns, one has become used to applying a certain backward pressure on the stick, assuming for the moment that the load is not or cannot be trimmed out. Until the habit of gently-banked turns is broken and the pilot thinks afresh about the theory of turning, he may not recognise that the steeper the turn the greater needs to be the backward pressure on the stick.

Another factor which determines the standard of turning accuracy is the frequency of monitoring the speed and balance of flight. The initial emphasis, in basic training, will certainly have been on attitude control, maybe to the exclusion of any reference to airspeed, with only occasional checking for slip or skid. Once a pilot is attempting to soar in thermals, he pays a lot of attention to the variometer reading, often to the detriment of lookout. All that is required is a pattern of scanning, striking the balance between lookout and other airmanship considerations, such as maintaining a good position relative to other gliders in the thermal, and an instrument scan, taking in the variometer reading, the airspeed, and the attitude and balance of flight (i.e. 'ball or string in the middle').

In soaring, however, airspeed will vary for a constant attitude when flying into and out of a thermal, and in some circumstances it may not be possible to maintain a constant attitude. With these provisos however, it is certain that much can be done to improve flying accuracy, but this requires the diagnosis of faults by timed turns and closer monitoring of instruments and then progressively extending oneself by setting closer tolerances and attempting progressively more difficult tasks.

If you can make accurate turns with 60° of bank, then turns with 45° of bank will require much less concentration. The ultimate aim is that flying accuracy itself should demand no more of one's concentration than does the functional side of driving a motor car.

Work-load

The remaining difficulty facing a pilot – and I am now thinking in the context of cross-country soaring – is resolving the work-load. Away from base, with a field landing imminent, one may be desperate to 'work the lift' found just before the firm commitment is made to land in the field. In this situation, concentration may be predominantly on the variometer, to the detriment of flying accuracy or indeed the relative position of the glider to the chosen field (critical in strong winds). At only four hundred feet, a certain balance must be struck between climbing and safety; what may be a comfortable circling speed at fifteen hundred feet is not necessary so at eight hundred feet. Even if an extra five knots on the speed is detrimental to the climb performance, it is better than spinning in.

Beware a situation which demands all of one's concentration on any one aspect of the flight.

In this situation, even the use of radio may reduce the concentration on handling accuracy (particularly on maintaining a safe speed) to a critical extent. Turning accuracy is therefore the key to successful soaring flight, and you will only develop the necessary skill by progressively extending yourself.

Speed control

The amount of emphasis placed on speed control in the past has not been sufficient for accurate flying of present-day gliders. The modern single-seater, and indeed the new generation of two-seaters, lack the 'feel' of gliders in days of yore; there is no airflow on your face and nothing like the amount of noise in the cockpit to give a good first approximation to speed. The problem is not unlike that facing a driver of a 1930s motor car converting to a good quality high-performance vehicle of the present day, in which speed monitoring becomes of some importance.

If one has been brought up with not much emphasis on speed monitoring or speed control, then the modern glider will prove difficult to fly until the emphasis has been changed. The remedy appears to be straightforward once one is conscious of the fault, but the two factors already mentioned – overcoming bad habits and the work-load problem – may reduce or preclude sufficient attention being paid to the airspeed indicator in certain phases of flight.

If hazardous situations are to be avoided, such as flying too slowly when low, with the risk of stalling or spinning, then how often the speed is monitored must take the situation into account. However long it might take to reduce the speed to a critical figure, and it is hardly conceivable that this will be less than a 'few seconds' in the worst case, then so long as the speed is monitored every 'few seconds', the glider will be flown safety. The exception perhaps is the gust-induced stall. The protection against this is flying with a higher speed than usual in turbulent conditions.

The basic scan already mentioned, of airspeed, variometer, attitude, and balance, should be altered to suit the circumstances.

The approach

The majority of solo pilots are unable to criticise their own approaches other than by the simple criteria of 'speed within limits' and 'landing in the right (chosen) place'. It might be argued that if these criteria are met, then the approach was a satisfactory one. Certain habitual shortcomings in technique, perception and judgement may however be revealed in making a difficult approach into a field. You will note that the approach rather than the landing itself is regarded as the difficult phase. The necessity therefore is to analyse the approach in a number of different ways; first the basic principles. The initial considerations for an approach are that an aiming point will be used and that this aiming point will, as a basic point of airmanship, be a 'safe distance' into the airfield or field. The glider will not touch down at the aiming point but 'float' some distance beyond it and the 'safe distance' is an allowance – a margin for error – in case the approach is misjudged.

Figure 1 shows the range of approach angles.

The argument in favour of making such an approach is based upon the safety margins available, that is if circumstances arise

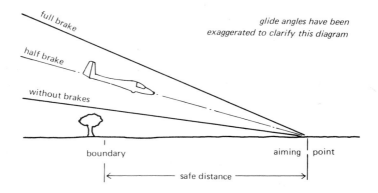

Figure 1. Range of approach angles.
a) The no-brake approach will be safe only inasmuch as the 'aiming point' (better termed the reference point, so as to discourage pilots from literally aiming the glider at it) is a fair distance into the field. This distance will depend on the height of obstructions and the length of the field. The latter is not usually critical on an airfield.

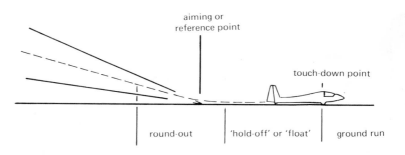

b) The reference point is not the point at which the glider actually lands, if speed has been maintained throughout the roundout, hold-off (float) and touchdown.

which change the approach, rising or sinking air, turbulence, curl-over (turbulence in the lee of a hill) or wind gradient, then the pilot can close or open the brakes to correct the situation. In practice, pilots only pay lip service to this theory of the half-brake approach because more often than not at the home airfield the margins for overshoot are enormous and for undershoot minimal, so that a more realistic assessment of this mid-range approach would be two-thirds brake.

The basic concept of the approach apart, however, it must be recognised that there are many variables which alter it. These, for the sake of simplicity, will be considered separately.

The position of the final turn
The factors which influence the position of the final turn are the performance of the glider in terms of glide angle and brake effect (as the example only considers one type of glider these factors can be ignored), the wind, and any side effects from it, such as turbulence, curl-over and wind gradient. For this example, the final turn will be considered to be complete by a height of 250 ft, although in practice it will often need to be higher and just occasionally lower. The respective positions of the final turn corresponding to no-brake, half-brake and full-brake are shown in Figure 2.

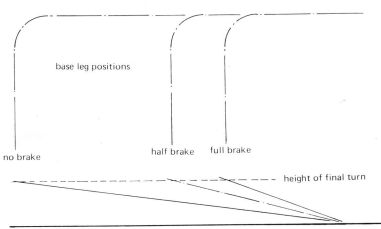

base leg positions

half brake   full brake

no brake

height of final turn

Figure 2. Range of base-leg positions. The position of these turns can be assumed to represent the no-wind case. If there were a wind then each of the turns would be correspondingly closer to the landing area.

Now in practice it will be found that the average pilot makes insufficient allowance for the effects of wind, and generally will not go far enough back when there is little or no wind, nor, on occasion, be close enough when the wind is fresh or strong. In terms of airbrake setting, this means that an approach in no wind is almost always made with full brake, and in strong winds with a small amount of brake, and since both of these approaches are nearer one limit than the other (i.e. full-brake/no-brake), then both represent a loss of safety margin. It should be recognised that the strong wind case may be influenced by the wind gradient which causes the glider to lose speed which, in the interest of regaining it (or not losing any more), needs a reduction in the airbrake setting. The effect of the wind gradient, while confusing the issue to some extent, should not be misinterpreted as being the only significant one in the strong wind case.

One factor which causes this lack of flexibility in positioning the base leg is the tendency for pilots to position the glider for the various phases of the circuit in relation to features on the ground. For the base leg or final turn, this may mean a position which is almost fixed irrespective of the conditions, with possible dire consequences the first time conditions outside previous experience are met.

The way to find out whether you suffer from this fault of rigid positioning of the base leg is to be conscious of the brake setting, or average brake setting, on each approach, but bear in mind that the analysis can only be made by studying your response on days with different wind strengths. It may help to ask someone, perhaps an instructor, to observe your approach and comment.

A slightly worse state of affairs arises if a pilot has poor perception in recognition of the possible undershoot or overshoot. You might well ask is it possible to recognise this fault in oneself? I believe it is – at least in a retrospective analysis. The analysis is best made in this instance not with regard to the average brake setting but regarding any necessary brake movement. Is progressive opening or progressive closing of the brakes required? If so, the consequences should be recognised. These circumstances are illustrated in Figure 3.

To complete the analysis it is necessary to look at some practical and psychological limitations which influence the pilot in his training and immediate post-solo flying. These contribute to the formation of habits and may persist even after they have been recognised. The first of these limitations relates to the tendency to 'cramp' the circuit.

There are several reasons for cramping the circuit, some justifiable and others less so. The first is perhaps trying to land too close to the airfield boundary; having dispensed with one safety margin – the undershoot area – the pilot, be he student or instructor, will not expose himself to a half-brake approach. Instead he retains the maximum possible margin by making a full-brake approach. The relevant psychological factors are well-developed instincts of self-preservation, notable in older pilots, and nervousness or a lack of confidence on the part of the instructor who, in addition, is not fully aware of his glider's performance.

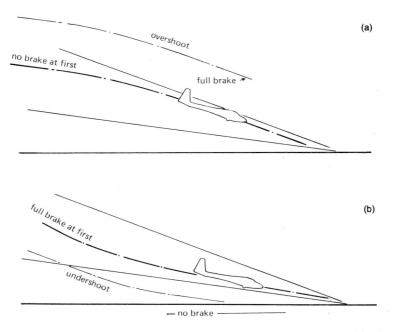

Figure 3. The effect of wind on actual approaches and changes of brake setting. If in light winds it is found that the brakes are being opened progressively to give an approach as shown at (a) or closed progressively as at (b) then this may well indicate poor perception. It is, of course, generally the undershoot case which is most critical and the observation is not entirely a relevant one if the cause is the wind gradient.

The extent of this pressure from psychological factors alone may extend in basic training to not allowing the student ever to make a low final turn. The end result is simple: the student becomes used to always opening the brakes as soon as the final turn is completed, often opening them fully. The habit of opening the airbrakes without thinking (and worse still, without perceiving) is then perpetuated. The risk of this habit being formed is perhaps at its greatest in gliders with spoilers rather than airbrakes when, instead of being used as a control to vary the approach as required, they become 'going-into-land levers'.

From the point of view both of instructing and of 'trouble shooting' one's own flying, it should be recognised that unless a moderate proportion – say more than thirty per cent – of approaches are flown without brakes to start with, then the risk of the habit existing is considerable. In any event a good approach, one that indicates the habit does not exist, would look like that in Figure 4.

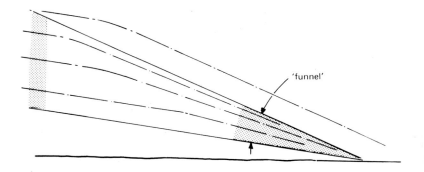

Figure 4. Avoiding opening the brakes without thinking. In each case shown the pilot does not open the brakes immediately the final turn is complete but sees first that the glider is going to overshoot.

A fundamental point – of great importance to instructors – arises here, which is that unless approaches are, in the main, within the funnel, it will be very difficult to analyse faults of brake-setting.

A further consequence of the too-high/too-close circumstance is equally serious; this point is to do with the speed-limiting capability of the brakes. The more powerful the brakes, the greater the risks of the habit forming. The normal way in which an approach is flown is that the speed is controlled with the elevator and the rate of descent (or the angle of approach, if you prefer) by the airbrakes. With very powerful brakes, it is possible to reverse this method of approach control by using the airbrakes in a speed-limiting capacity and 'pointing' the glider where you want to land – or more usually at the aiming point. The method is perfectly acceptable as a means of landing in the right place after getting a circuit wrong – perhaps too cramped in a field landing case. But to carry out such approaches regularly has the risk of learning an approach technique suitable only for gliders with powerful airbrakes. If this is true of the basic training gliders – two-seaters and the first single-seaters – then it is quite likely that a pilot has a habit of which he is completely unaware. He will only discover it when he flies a glider with less powerful brakes and by this time the habit will be firmly established. The diagram, Figure 5, summarises the relevant factors.

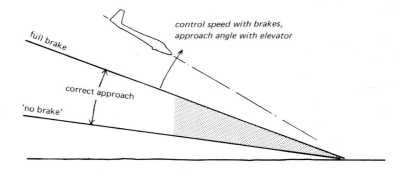

Figure 5. Elevator controls speed, and brake controls approach angle, or vice versa. Above the full-brake line the risks are of controlling the speed with brakes and approach angle with elevator. The important point to appreciate is that the pilot may not be aware of this habit.

The requirement is to arrive within the approach funnel more often than not so that the need to use airbrakes to limit the speed can be avoided.

Even if this criterion is met, there is still some difficulty in analysing an approach and saying whether or not it is satisfactory. This arises because a student must be allowed some tolerance on approach speed; for example, an approach which starts at 52 knots and ends at 58 (just prior to the round out) or the reverse will have achieved an average of 55 knots, which was perhaps the speed stipulated. In both cases, the fault may be due to poor co-ordination between elevator and airbrake, with the nose not lowered sufficiently as the brakes are opened, or raised as they are closed again. The critical case is where speed is lost; is it due to too large a brake setting or the nose not being lowered enough? This is a fine point of interpretation, especially if the landing area is a large one and the student has not nominated the landing point.

The collective faults which constitute poor approach technique are:

1.   Not making sufficient allowance for different wind strengths in the positioning of the final turn. Try to be aware of the average airbrake setting. Is the amount small in strong winds and large in light winds?

2.   Opening the airbrakes without thinking, due to being too close too often.

3.   Not approaching within the 'funnel' and so being at risk of using a different (and wrong) technique, controlling the speed with the brakes, something which only works in gliders with powerful brakes.

4.   Inability to recognise the undershoot because it has never occurred, or been demonstrated.

It should be your aim always to make approaches within the funnel with an appropriate and a moderate brake setting and a high standard of speed control.

The circuit

The old maxim that 'a good landing is preceded by a good approach and a good approach by a good circuit' is often confirmed in practice. It follows that poor technique and bad habits in the approach phase often stem from faults in circuit planning. This is not surprising when you consider that many training circuits may be too similar, either because the instructor does not contrive enough variation, or because the launch height (by winch or autotow) and the conditions are very much the same. Whatever the reason for the similarity, the result is that the student does not have an appreciation of the factors which should alter the circuit.

As with the approach, we will assume that certain things are constant, in order to simplify the analysis. In this case it is the height at which the circuit is started – assumed to be 800 ft. If this is so then the factors which will cause the position at which the circuit is commenced to vary are:

1. The length of the airfield.
2. The strength of the wind.
3. The amount of cross-wind.

The one variable not considered is the variation in training gliders; it is assumed that one type is being used throughout basic training.

The length of the airfield
This factor is best considered in the context of an airfield with runways of different lengths. The only further assumption must be that the landing area in each case bears the same relationship to the end of each runway and the wind strength is the same in each case.

In the event, if the downwind leg is to be of the same length and entail the same height loss then the relative starting positions must be different in each case when related to the upwind end of each runway; this is shown in Figure 6.

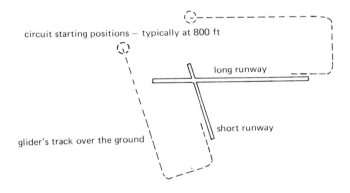

Figure 6. Effect of length of airfield on starting position of circuit. In the case of the short runway (3,000 ft) the starting position will be upwind of the upwind end and for the long runway (6,000 ft) downwind of the upwind end; for a runway length between these two (4,500 ft) the starting position might be the upwind end.

How often is the only interpretation on this starting position 'at the upwind end of the runway'?

Wind strength

To appreciate the effect of the wind, think of a single-runway airfield and different wind strengths – no wind and moderately strong wind. In either case, if the height at which the circuit is started is to be the same then the same criteria of distance/time and height-loss on the downwind leg apply. In the case of a strong wind the starting position should be well upwind of that in the no-wind case, as shown in Figure 7.

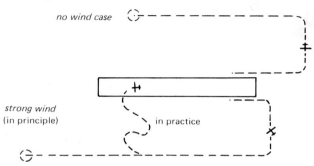

Figure 7. Effect of wind strength on starting position of circuit. There is one other factor that influences the length of the downwind leg and that is the distance behind the landing area that the base leg is positioned.

The practical problem that arises in the strong wind case is when the glider has been launched by winch (or car) and cannot actually get far enough upwind to the ideal circuit starting position, and the risk with a short downwind leg is of overshooting the turn onto base leg.

So two factors influence the starting position of the circuit in relation to the upwind end of the runway; a third factor relates to the amount of any cross-wind component. To allow for this, the starting position is moved nearer to, or further away from, the runway so as to give the same amount of time and therefore height loss on the base leg because the base leg will be flown with either a head-wind or a tail-wind component. The next diagram, Figure 8, summarises the factors which influence the starting position for the circuit.

Failure to make these adjustments in circuit flying at one's home airfield, or even to recognise them, leads to problems with eventual field landings when the circuit may *actually* be started at the upwind end of the chosen field rather than several fields upwind – the number obviously depending on the size of the fields.

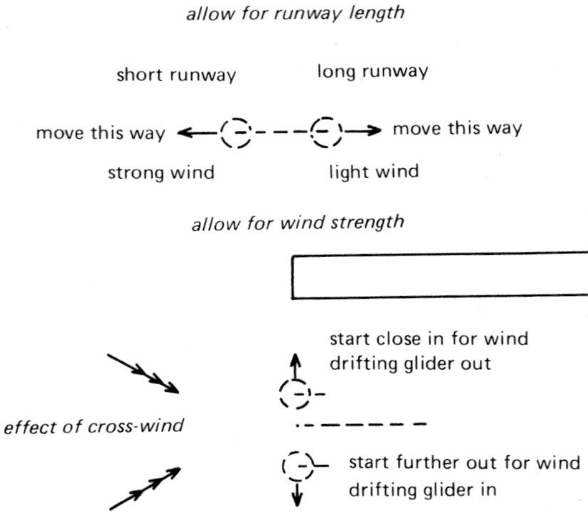

allow for runway length

short runway   long runway

move this way ◄—(⁀ͦ‿)‑ ‑ ‑(⁀ͦ‿)—► move this way

strong wind   light wind

allow for wind strength

start close in for wind
drifting glider out

effect of cross-wind

start further out for wind
drifting glider in

Figure 8. Effect of cross-wind on starting position of circuit. While these variations may be dealt with in other ways – notably different heights at which the circuit is started – the main concern is that pilots are aware of the need for these adjustments.

The final point on circuit flying relates to the position of the base leg which has already been dealt with in considering the position of the final turn.

It is assumed throughout the above section that height has remained adequate throughout the circuit and there was no need to turn in early because the glider was running out of height. These considerations are of course fundamental to basic training and should not need to be raised in the context of examining and improving one's skill for cross-country flying.

The landing

The final phase of flight which should be looked at is the landing. It might seem that there are not enough variations in the way in which a glider can be landed to warrant consideration but consider the definition of a good landing. Usually it will be described as 'fully held off'. What does this constitute?

'Fully held off' is usually taken to mean keeping the glider airborne as long as possible, until, in fact, it stalls on to the ground. If this is the only criterion then the sort of landing which results is one in which the tail skid (or tail wheel) touches the ground first and the glider pitches (sometimes heavily) on to its main wheel. This sort of landing is not particularly comfortable and is often actively discouraged in basic training. Instead, what is done is to attempt to 'hold off fully' but with the main wheel sufficiently close to the ground to avoid this pitching on to it. The consequence is that the touch-down speed is a knot or two higher than it would be in the 'fully held off' case.

However, once a touch-down speed a couple of knots in excess of the stall is usual, a higher speed may be accepted and the landings may then be described as 'flown on'; that is the glider is deliberately put on the ground at a speed some knots in excess of the stall. This practice, like many others, can become a habit; what is needed is an awareness of variation in technique and as a refinement use of the method most appropriate to the circumstance:

1.   Flying on to the ground and using the wheel brake on a smooth surface.
2.   Holding off fully (even the extreme case of pitching heavily on to the main wheel) on a rough surface will minimise the risk of damage to the undercarriage and also help to dissipate some of the glider's energy.

These variations apart, there are other landing considerations and they are to do with landing uphill (if the ground slopes down more steeply than the glider's full-brake glide angle, landing is impossible). Two difficulties arise:

1.   The glider will have to change its flight path (at round-out) more than it would do for a landing on the level.
2.   The perspective of the field may delude one into thinking that it is being overshot, resulting in more brake being used with the risk of causing an undershoot.

The note of caution for an uphill landing is that speed will have to be maintained right down to round-out height and that the round-out may need to be started sooner than usual.

One final point to make is particularly relevant to modern gliders, which often have poor aileron control at low speed – certainly much worse than typical club gliders. To keep the wings level in the final stages of the ground run will require much more concentration and anticipation on the part of the pilot. Failure to concentrate is often the cause of ground loops, a common hazard even in quite short crops.

Sideslipping
It may seem odd that this manoeuvre, a supplementary means of approach control, is only a post-solo exercise, and then infrequently taught, when in some countries it is taught prior to solo. The reason for this is obscure. It might be due to the fact that most of the British-built gliders had airbrakes which were powerful enough to make sideslipping unnecessary, but this can only be part of it. Nevertheless, there are occasions when the ability to sideslip will be very useful, and so full consideration of the manoeuvre, its limitations and any risks in doing it is warranted.

What is a sideslip?
The terms slipping and skidding are normally used in the context of a turn; slipping is inwards towards the lower wing and skidding outwards towards the higher one. While the deliberate slipping turn is also a very useful manoeuvre, it is the straight sideslip as a means of steepening the approach that will be considered first.

If at any time the glider is made to slip by the deliberate application of rudder, it may be said to be sideslipping. However the deliberate manoeuvre requires the use of all three controls. If rudder alone is applied – when the glider is flying straight – the initial effect (known usually as primary) will be to yaw the glider, but soon after it will start to turn, albeit in an unbalanced manner. This is due to the various aerodynamic effects due to the differing airflows over each wing and the effect of dihedral; both these cause the glider to roll. A deliberate sideslip will counteract the secondary effects of rudder, the glider being constrained to fly in a straight line. This may be achieved with the glider's wings level or banked; the more the bank the steeper the sideslip and the greater the height loss.

The sideslip is started by the application of rudder in one direction (say left) and a progressive application of bank to the right so that the glider continues to fly in a straight line in the direction of approach. Being flown sideways to some extent increases the drag, and the glide angle is steepened. This state of affairs is not a stable one; the glider's nose tends to lower, and for a controlled sideslip the elevator must be used to stop this. The amount of this backward pressure on the stick varies with the type of glider and the steepness of the sideslip.

Before considering the manoeuvre as a means of approach control, a particular limitation must be examined. A progressively steepening sideslip will have rudder gradually applied (the rate will be dealt with later) and the wing progressively lowered to keep the glider flying along its approach path; the limit is reached when full rudder has been applied. If one attempts to steepen the descent rate further by applying more bank, the glider will not maintain a straight path but will start to turn towards the lower wing because the weather-cocking effect is greater than the rudder power can combat. It is important that this limit is recognised and experienced because it is the point at which the manoeuvre goes wrong and some of the risks arise (see p. 36). To appreciate the range of approach control that this manoeuvre offers, its limits must be considered. The minimum effective sideslip would be with full rudder applied and the wings maintained level (some aileron will be necessary to counter secondary effects); the maximum is determined by the power of the rudder to counteract the weathercock stability. Whatever the extent of the sideslip in practice, the approach path (i.e. track over the ground) would have to be held. However, the angle of sideslip can be varied to give a degree of directional control, as Figures 9–12 below illustrate.

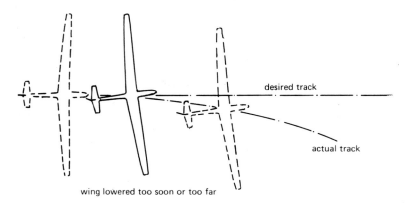

desired track

actual track

wing lowered too soon or too far

Figure 9. Sideslipping. Too much bank.
Nose to the left; right wing lowered but too much for the yaw. The glider starts to track to the right. The fault developed because the wing was lowered too far too soon for the amount of rudder applied, or, insufficient rudder was used.

This situation may be redeemed by reducing the bank angle.

In contrast, the opposite situation arises if insufficient bank is used. The correct approach track may be regained by increasing the angle of bank.

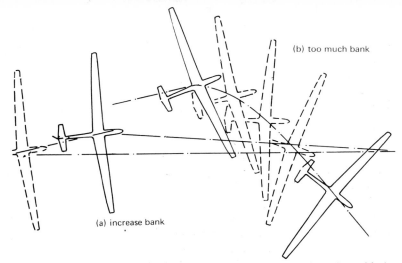

(b) too much bank

(a) increase bank

Figure 10. Sideslipping. Slipping to the left (left wing down, right rudder).
If the extra bank is applied soon enough, at (a), a new approach track can be achieved. If the glider is allowed to get too far off the ideal approach line and the bank has to be increased beyond the limiting angle, as at (b), then a turn will commence and the sideslip will be out of control.

If a degree of directional control is to be retained then the tracks of the limits of sideslip (i.e. no bank to limiting bank) must be visualised relative to the approach line, as shown in the next figure.

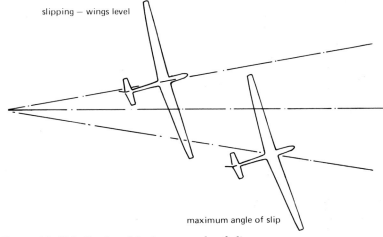

slipping — wings level

maximum angle of slip

Figure 11. Sideslipping. Maximum angle of slip.
If the maximum angle of slip is along the approach line then there is no possibility of a correction (to the right in this case) being made by further increasing the bank angle. In this instance, it would be necessary to come out of the sideslip and re-enter it differently orientated, as shown in Figure 12.

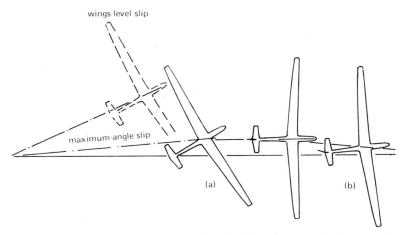

wings-level slip

maximum-angle slip

(a)

(b)

Figure 12. Sideslipping. Correction when bank angle cannot be increased.
The glider will be taken out of the sideslip at (a) and re-entered at (b) with
the nose yawed less to the left of track.

*If the sideslip is required as the main means of approach control
(perhaps the brakes are jammed), then it is desirable that directional
adjustments can also be made without coming out of the sideslip. In
other words, the pilot must be able to make these adjustments while
adjusting the approach, making it steeper or less steep as required.*

Based on this assumption, the approach can now be considered
solely in terms of achieving the desired approach angle. The shallowest angle will be achieved with the wings-level slip and the
maximum with the full sideslip (when anything steeper would make
the weathercock stability cause the glider to turn). The range of
approach control is shown in Figure 13.

The sideslip therefore is a useful supplementary means of
approach control and would be the sole means in a glider without
airbrakes (or spoilers) or where the control becomes jammed.
There is however a case where the ability to carry out the manoeuvre is highly desirable and that is where the glider has been
positioned too close to a field. In this position, a full-brake approach
would result in an overshoot and this situation may occur in a glider
with less effective brakes than the pilot has been used to, or if he is
apprehensive about the field landing and so 'crowds' the circuit.
Here the sideslip is essential if a landing is to be made in the chosen

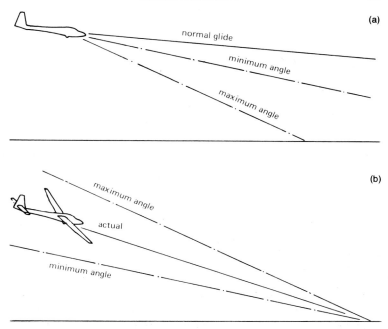

Figure 13. Sideslipping. Glide-path correction.
In approach control terms (assuming no airbrakes), the pilot would need to
position the glider approximately mid-way between maximum and
minimum sideslip paths (a), so that the actual approach would be as shown
at (b), and in this position there would be the potential to correct for an
overshoot by increasing the sideslip or an undershoot by decreasing it. The
pilot must still be able to adjust the direction in either case.

field; by using it the pilot gets the glider within the range of the
brakes' control capability. The sequence of events starts with the
recognition that the glider will overshoot – even with full brake. A
sideslip, with some brake if necessary, is carried out until the glider
is lower on the glide path and it can be recognised that it could
undershoot if full brake were used for the rest of the approach. This
should be perceived by continuing to fly with full brake after stopping the sideslip. If enough height has not been lost then a further
sideslip should be made.

The advantages of carrying out the sideslip at the height in excess
of two hundred feet or so, are that if it is less than perfectly exe-
cuted then there is still time to get the speed and heading correct.

Directional or heading control has already been dealt with; speed control raises other problems.

Speed control in the sideslip

As in every phase of flight, the speed is controlled by the elevator, but in many gliders the air speed indicator will misread in the sideslip and may be quite useless. Speed control therefore must be by 'feel' of the glider and its controls. The co-ordination requirement is gradually to apply a backward pressure on the stick as the sideslip is entered and to relax the backward pressure on coming out of the sideslip. On entry if the pressure is applied late, then the speed will be too high; on recovery if the backward pressure is relaxed too soon, speed will build up, and if too late, speed will be lost. Neither of the recovery alternatives is satisfactory because, in the first case, the field may be overshot and in the second, the glider may be stalled and land heavily. One particular feature of the sideslip, which worries many pilots, is the risk of stalling if too much backward pressure is applied to the stick. To appreciate the degree of risk, it is worthwhile trying to stall the glider during a sideslip – not of course near the ground. The majority of gliders will not have sufficient elevator power to bring the glider to the point of stall and those that do will recover instantly the backward pressure is relaxed.

If entry and recovery have the correct elevator co-ordination the the speed after the sideslip will be the same as that before the entry and it is this level of skill that a pilot must strive to achieve before the manoeuvre can be used to extend the glider's range of approach control.

Other safety considerations

In addition to the risks relating to speed control – or the lack of it – there is a real hazard in continuing the sideslip down to ground level; the 'break-off' height is really determined by the ability of the pilot. The height required to establish a steady approach, if the recovery is less than ideal, will depend on whether airbrakes are being used at the time and, if so, how far they are open. For early attempts at this exercise (after dual instruction of course) a hundred feet or so ensures safety. An additional proviso is that any time directional control is lost the practice should be abandoned. With improving skill, the manoeuvre may be continued to a lower height.

A useful practice in the recovery is to come out of the sideslip very gradually. Carried to its logical conclusion, this will have the glider still sideslipping as it reaches ground level – but before touch-down and with the wings now level. Immediately prior to touch-down, it is necessary to centralise the rudder – equivalent to 'kicking off the drift'; the manoeuvre continued to this limit would of course be necessary in the event of brake failure.

Another hazard in sideslipping is the operation of the rudder; on commencing the sideslip a pressure – often considerable – will have to be applied to deflect the rudder. Once the manoeuvre is stabilised however, the air loads on the rudder may hold it in the fully-deflected position; this state is known as 'over-locking'. To return the rudder to its central position requires a force on the opposite pedal, whereas in normal flight all that is required is a relaxation of the original force. In order to emphasise this point, consider a sideslip to the right, that is nose to the left (left rudder and right wing down); to recover, if the rudder is locked over, will require a force to be applied to the right rudder pedal rather than relaxing the pressure on the left.

The problem will arise if the pilot is unaware of this state and delay occurs in recovery from the sideslip because, having relaxed the pressure on the pedal, an additional force is required on the other pedal and the pilot is slow to recognise this need. The defence against this hazard is to establish, at height, whether the rudder locks over or not by slipping as steeply as possible and taking the appropriate foot off the rudder pedal to see whether the pedal (and the rudder) stays in the same place.

Surprisingly, the majority of pilots regard sideslipping as a hazardous exercise. Being shown how to do it and practising it a few times soon bring them to a level of competence that makes spot landings without using airbrakes a distinct possibility. No pilot should regard himself as skilled unless he can sideslip his glider. Practice breeds confidence and a truly skilful pilot takes pride in his ability.

In conclusion, one's flying skill can always be improved. The motivation to do so however may only come after the need has arisen. A detailed understanding and an analysis of the way in which various manoeuvres are carried out is the best step towards this improvement. The second is having a purpose for every flight.

2 Purpose for Every Flight

Once a pilot is solo there is a gradually decreasing involvement with instructors; after daily flying checks, progress checks are the only contact. During this phase, a student's flying may not progress for several reasons:

1. Lack of contact and hence direction from instructors.
2. Lack of opportunity to extend himself due to launching limitations, and or lack of opportunity to soar.
3. Lack of initiative, because of training circumstances, to do other than go up, around and down.

In such circumstances, it is not surprising that a student does not progress. The system of check flights does not do much to help; they will determine a minimum level of skill in dealing with so-called emergencies but little to raise the standard of flying and skill. If there is little further instruction, then the pilot is left to improve himself – a difficult enough task in all conscience.

If the ultimate goal is to become a soaring pilot and eventually go across country, then there is a limit to the steps which can be taken in this direction just by local flying. But the student is constrained to fly locally by the rules and regulations and so a 'Catch 22' situation arises. What is needed is an awareness of the steps that can improve skills within the constraints imposed. Some of the possibilities are given below.

1. *Soaring in thermals.* Searching, finding, centring and using as efficiently as possible.
2. *Navigation.* Relating features on the ground and symbols on the map, map orientation, a sense of distance related to visibility and a sense of direction or orientation using the sun and a compass to assist. (See Chapter 4.)

3. *Glider performance.* An awareness of how far the glider will
    travel from a given height and the effect of wind, the right
    speed to fly in given circumstances. (See Chapter 6.)
4. *Field selection.* An awareness of field size and state, the type
    and length of crop and seasonal variations. (See Chapter 5.)
5. *Field landings.* An awareness of circuit size in relation to the
    number of fields flown over, obstructions of any sort, and the
    difficulty of identifying crops. (See Chapter 5.)

Such a list, at first sight, seems formidable, but with a little
thought it is not difficult to contrive exercises incorporating some of
the possibilities. One of the simplest teaches a little about gliders'
performance.

Exercise 1
For a given height of launch – usually a winch or autotow – decide
how much height you can lose gliding into wind and allow an
adequate margin for return and circuit. Use local ground features to
confirm the distance. Some simple sums are advisable before
attempting this exercise.

Suppose the launch height is 1,300 feet, and the circuit must be
started at 700 feet; the height available for the exercise is 600 feet.
If the wind is 20 knots and the glider is to be flown into it at 50 knots,
the ground speed will be 30 knots; on the return the ground speed
will be 60 knots if the glider is flown at a speed of 40. Based on the
ratio of these speeds, the height that can be lost in gliding into wind
is two-thirds of the total available – 400 feet in this case. There is no
allowance for the height loss in the turn but then you can always
abandon the exercise if your nerve gives out. The exercise is 'fail
safe' in that you can always turn in early on the circuit which in itself
is worthwhile practice. It should be noted that this exercise is
essentially one for a non-soaring day.

The background knowledge essential to this exercise is the speed
at which the glider should be flown for maximum distance when
flying into or down wind. Into wind, a rough guide is to add one-
third of the wind speed to the best glide speed; down wind the best
speed will be between the minimum sink speed (see Fig. 48, p. 139)
and the best glide speed – the stronger the wind the nearer the
speed will be to the minimum sink speed.

It would be quite a good idea to get a glide calculator even at this stage of your experience. A simple one like the JSW local-soaring calculator will do nicely. (*Note:* A JSW best-glide 1-in-23 calculator (1 in 23 being typical for a club solo glider, a K8 or Swallow) gives a speed of 50 knots for flying into a 20-knot wind, and a 400-feet height loss corresponds to 0.82 miles flown; for a tail wind of 20 knots, the speed to fly is 38 knots and for a 200-feet height loss, the distance covered will be better than 1.1 miles. The discrepancy from the previous sum arises of course because of the different sink rates at the two speeds.)

There are some logical developments to this exercise but these fall more appropriately under the heading of local soaring. A second exercise, with much more scope, was also originally conceived as a winter-time exercise.

Exercise 2

This exercise requires a high aerotow to, say, four thousand feet. It is the sort of thing that an instructor can persuade a student to do so long as he is convincing about the benefits.

Our basic glider, with a 1-in-23 glide angle will (from the calculator) glide 15.5 nm from 4,000 feet, almost 4 nm per 1,000 feet; with a 10-knot tail wind, the distance becomes 19½ nm.

The exercise consists in towing the glider to a point a certain distance upwind – the height and distance to suit the circumstances. The safety margin, that is the height at which the glider gets back to the field, can be as much as 2,000 feet for the first try; this figure is reduced as confidence is gained. The plan for the flight should be outlined as in Figure 14.

The briefing

The briefing will need to be more or less comprehensive, depending on the confidence and knowledge level of the pilot; the following list should be used as a guide. Extract from it the relevant items.

1.   *The point of release.* There is a need for the pilot to orientate himself. The minimum requirement is to make a 180° turn after the tow out but this may not be achieved if the pilot turns immediately he releases from tow. He can be helped by:

   (a)   The tug pilot orbiting a couple of times so that the student sees the direction in which he returns.

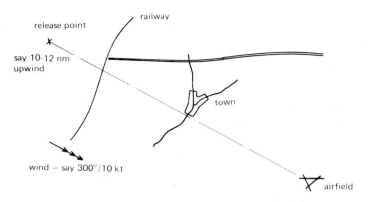

Figure 14a. High aerotow and long glide to appreciate the glider's performance. The glider should be towed to a position some 12 nm upwind. On the glide back the calculator can be used to check the actual height needed at a couple of suitable features, at known distance – reading the height required off the inner scale (Figure 14b and page 62).

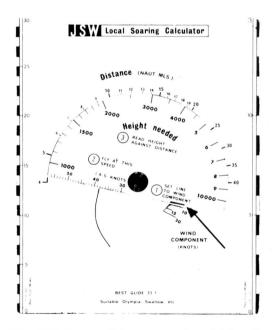

Figure 14b. The JSW Soaring Calculator set for a 10-kt tail-wind.

few hundred feet or so – and that you have some idea about the shape of this rising air and perhaps its structure. Both of these factors, shape and structure of thermals (see page 56), have a bearing on the techniques used to climb in them, and there are several practical points which support the theory.

The starting point, for the purpose of this explanation, assumes that a thermal has already been found but that the glider is not centred in it. The glider will be centred on the basis of variometer readings, and sensations, by making adjustments to the circle. The situation considered in Figure 15 is a hypothetical one and may seldom occur in exactly the way illustrated.

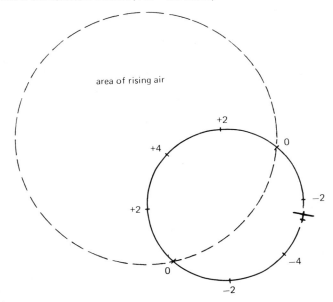

rates of climb/descent in knots (1 kt = 100 ft/min)

Figure 15. Thermal centring – in the 'edge' of the thermal.
In this diagram the edge of the rising air mass is defined as the point at which the variometer would be reading zero. Strictly therefore the air is rising at the same rate the glider is sinking; this state of affairs is usually termed 'zero sink'. The other assumptions for the moment are that there is no lag or delay in the variometer indicating the glider's rate of descent or ascent and that the glider is making a steady circle – that is one at near constant speed and angle of bank; features of the thermal itself which tend to alter these last two points will be considered separately.

Having made these assumptions some variometer readings around this circle (or series of circles) can be considered – see Figure 15. If you have had some experience of thermals then you will agree that this situation is idealised, but certain principles have to be established for interpreting variometer readings; in this case the best or worse readings given an indication of where the best lift lies. On their own, the variometer readings are useless; it is the glider's heading – the direction in which it is flying – when these readings occur that matters. If the pilots is to appreciate this then he must be orientated – conscious of the glider's position in terms of compass headings N, S, E and W, or more usually in relation to the sun or features on the ground. With orientation, the worst/best variometer readings become known as worst/best headings and in this example it does not matter which is used because they give the same information.

The first practical point to be made is relation to this circle or any other is this:

It is better to make a shift of the circle based on evidence of at least two previous circles in which the variometer readings are the same or approximately so.

This is because the circles themselves and disturbances in the rising air may not give a clear or true indication of where the best lift lies (relative to the circles already flown).

If the conditions are so turbulent as to preclude two consecutive circles with the same readings, the evidence from one will have to do. It is only after the variometer reading has started to improve or worsen that one is aware of what was the worst or best heading. Also the glider must turn through 270° after the best heading, and fly through the sink again, which may be thought undesirable. Finally, it might be argued in the case in Figure 15, that the evidence of each half circle – one in sink the other in lift – corroborates the other.

In the midst of all this head-in-cockpit activity, remember to keep a good look-out.

'Shifting' the circle, or 'centring'

The next obvious requirement is to move the circle towards the centre of the lift. In principle this is done by straightening up, as shown in Figure 16.

Work-load considerations apart, another factor may be significant. Assume for the moment that the circle should be moved

Assuming the final shift (c) in Figure 17 above has centred the glider, the only further adjustment would be to vary the angle of bank (generally increasing it gradually) but more about the angle of bank later.

What is the optimum angle of bank?

Pilots rarely agree on the optimum angle of bank to use in a thermal; however, personal preferences apart, the significant factors are:

1. The limiting angle of bank at which the pilot can turn the glider consistently – it is no use doing turns at 45° of bank if they go wrong frequently.
2. Theoretical considerations based on the structure of the thermal and the circling performance of the glider (how slowly it can be flown and its sink rate at various bank angles) show that there is quite a wide tolerance in bank angle – from 25° to 50° – which will give similar climb rates.

The compromise is the combination of the variables – speed and bank angle – which give the best climb rate. Words of advice the majority of inexperienced soaring pilots would do well to heed are: 'Be flexible, and experiment with bank angles to see whether climb performance can be improved.' Confirm bank angles at given speeds by timed turns rather than rely on subjective impressions. Some pilots put Chinagraph pencil marks on the canopy, which provide an equally useful guide.

The following table may be useful in this respect:

Speed (kt)	Radius of turn (ft)			Time for 360° (secs)		
	40	45	50	40	45	50
Bank angle						
20°	392	496	613	36·4	41·0	45·6
30°	247	313	386	22·9	25·8	28·7
40°	170	215	266	15·7	17·8	19·8
45°	—	181	223	—	14·9	16·6

Now back to the practical problems of centring in thermals. The theory of centring technique so far considered has to be expanded before it is of practical value. Before doing so it is important to understand some features of the variometer for which one must make allowance.

Total-energy systems

A 'basic' variometer indicates the rate at which the glider is ascending or descending. The principle on which it works is measuring the rate of change of air density. Air density decreases as the glider climbs and increases as it descends.

To help understand the principles consider the following:

1. If the air in which the glider is flying is neither rising nor descending then the rate of sink indicated by the variometer is that of the glider at that speed – say 1·2 kt – a typical value.
2. If the glider is flying in air which is rising at 4 kt, then this will cause the glider to climb at $4 - 1·2 = 2·8$ kt. If 4 kt is indicated on the vario then the air is actually rising at 5·2 kt $(4 + 1·2)$ assuming the glider's speed to be the same as before.
3. With a simple variometer system (i.e. not a total-energy one), if the glider is climbing at an indicated 4 kt and the speed is increased (while still in the same rising air) then the rate of climb indicated will reduce and so will the actual rate of climb of course. This is because the glider's sink rate will be greater at this new speed. Conversely if the speed is reduced a greater climb rate will be indicated for some time.

As speed variations are to some extent inevitable this makes it difficult to decide where the best lift lies and what is needed is a system which eliminates indications due solely to speed changes. This is the total-energy system. The compensation is achieved by a connection from the pitot which measures the dynamic pressure (due to the glider's speed) into the variometer system.

A total energy system can be checked by diving and climbing the glider and seeing whether there are any changes in the variometer reading other than those appropriate to the normal changes in sink rate at the various speeds.

A good total energy system makes soaring relatively easy.

Variometer 'lag'

The delay in the instrument presenting the actual rate of climb or descent varies with the type of instrument – electrical or mechanical – and various features of the system which are beyond the scope of this book. There is no reason why a modestly priced variometer, as is found in typical club gliders, should not be quite adequate for all practical purposes. Such an instrument will have a lag time of up to

The whole combined process of centring requires a pilot to build up a picture in his mind of where the best lift lies. Figure 19 shows a method which in effect combines worst heading, best heading and surge.

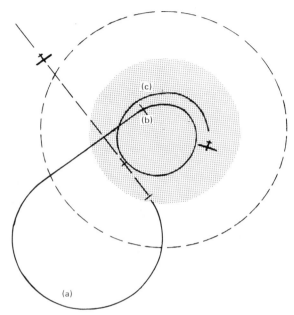

Figure 19. Thermal centring – using the 'surges'.
(a)   Moderate angle of bank during the first turn to establish the lift pattern.
(b)   Tighten turn by increasing the bank angle soon after the surge is felt.
(c)   Angle of bank reduced to improve climb rate (the opposite of tightening it from the medium turn.

Searching for thermals

For the pilot launched by winch or autotow to a limited height, the time and area of search are also limited. A known good thermal source is an obvious choice and good ground features will include runways, corn fields, and wind shadow areas, the latter often combined with south- or sunward-facing slopes. The frustration element for the pilot is that however good the thermal source, it does not give off a continuous supply and so one can frequently be unlucky.

To improve the chances of contacting lift, any signs of it, such as cloud forming towards the upwind end of the field or, obviously, other gliders circling, should be taken into account. One particular clue appropriate to light-wind days is the sudden rush of air, a wind of random direction, which follows the start of a thermal. If you are desperate to get away – for a 300-kilometre attempt, say – it may pay to wait until the signs are favourable.

The next consideration of importance is when some lift has been found. The priorities are staying with the lift and getting established rather than achieving the maximum rate of climb as quickly as possible. The characteristics of the thermal in its initial stage should be considered; an enormous mass of air with considerable inertia has to accelerate and this will take some time. A bubbling, turbulent sort of feeling is the first sign, and there may be a large area in which the glider does not sink but does not climb either. In this circumstance, it is better to stay in the same area making gentle turns and waiting for the thermal to get going.

Realise that it may be twenty minutes before the next thermal comes from this source and the next nearest thermal may be a mile of two away. Patience and perseverance are the two most important requirements.

Once the glider has started to climb, do not be in too much of a hurry to get centred until a few hundred feet have been gained – unless of course you are really confident of the thermal's position. The structure of the thermal in the lower levels of the atmosphere up to the height of the gradient wind has some significance in terms of centring technique. It must be assumed that the thermal will be influenced by the wind as it breaks away from the ground; if there is any wind gradient, then this, plus the thermal's inertia, will mean that it will drift over the ground at an increasing rate as it rises through the gradient. The effective limit of the wind gradient is the height at which the wind is no longer influenced by friction as it passes over the ground; this height is generally regarded as being two thousand feet over land. So, up to this height, the thermal drifts with the wind and effectively 'leans' in a downwind direction; above two thousand feet the only effect will be relative changes in the wind (strength and direction) including wind shear effects which often break up the thermals.

That the thermal leans is significant because the glider is continuously descending and 'falling out' of the downwind side of it. If the lift is lost or deteriorates, it will usually be possible to find it or re-centre it by straightening into wind. Often it will be necessary to fly straight for much longer than would be necessary in re-centring the thermal at greater heights.

Persistence is therefore important in getting away from low down, either from a launch or from a 'low scrape' on a cross-country flight. With more height to spare, say from an aerotow launch, the choice of lift source, from cloud or ground clues, and the chances of getting away are increased considerably.

One of the first decisions facing a pilot on an aerotow is when or whether to pull off as the glider is towed through a thermal. The decision is quite a difficult one for the inexperienced pilot, and having released a few times at 1,200 feet or thereabouts and having 'fallen down', it is likely that the full 2,000 feet will be taken. It will not always be the case that the tug pilot manages to put you in a thermal at exactly this height, and it is probably better to release from 1,600 feet upwards when a strong thermal is encountered. To appreciate its strength you will need to know the normal climb rate of the combination (tug plus glider) otherwise there may be a risk of misinterpreting flying out of sinking air as flying into a thermal.

If a thermal was not encountered during the course of the tow, then it may not be a particularly good soaring day, or the pilot has towed you to an area devoid of likely clouds. In either case, you must decide whether to continue on tow in the hope that a thermal will be encountered, or release and decide where to go and find the lift. This searching phase is critical; even from an aerotow the height and time to find the lift are limited. The approach to finding a thermal is better if it is a positive one.

The first possibility, and one that many pilots resort to, is to 'float around' in the hope that a thermal will find them or they will blunder into one. A thermal found in this way is as good as any in terms of staying airborne but an important part of cross-country flying is choosing the next likely source of lift. If the thermal finds you, then an opportunity to develop your sky-reading ability has been lost. There are a number of 'do's and don'ts' for the searching phase of a soaring flight.

DO

1.   Make a definite choice of cloud, go to it and search underneath; make wide turns to cover a reasonable area.

2.   In flying towards the cloud, fly the glider positively, that is, choose a point to fly towards and do not let the glider wander about, letting it be turned by lift under one wing for example. Imperceptible amounts can be significant.

3.   Persist with the search; as the thermal goes higher it gets bigger and the core may be progressively more difficult to find. Even different values of sink may give a clue to the direction in which the core lies.

DON'T

1.   Give up after one or two turns unless the cloud is obviously 'dying' (more strictly, evaporating), a sure sign that the lift has ceased.

2.   Give up because the thermal is not as strong as you expected. The day may not be quite as good as it looked and the same requirements are relevant as in the first thermal off a winch launch (see page 53).

The characteristics of the thermal, especially on entering it, will not be so marked as they might have been lower down. The physical sensations of the surge, with its tendency to increase the speed and even pitch the glider nose up, may not be at all obvious. At height there will be more entrained air – that is air which is being dragged up by the thermal itself. This air too will be rising, but not at any great rate, and it is often the case that an inexperienced pilot will start to circle at the first indications of rising air (which may be entrained air). If this comes to nothing – that is, there is no obvious centre and the air is slightly or moderately turbulent – then this is probably what has happened and the centre of the thermal is still some distance away.

In this context, one of the theories of thermal structure, and to my mind the most valid, is the 'doughnut' or vortex ring theory; this is shown in Figure 20.

The vortex ring theory is borne out in practice by a couple of points:

1.   The tendency of the lower gliders in a thermal to catch up the ones above (a safety point to remember when cloud flying).

2.   That it is possible to join below other gliders without finding thermal lift at all, implying that even if the thermal is a column of air, it must eventually cease to be supplied with rising air.

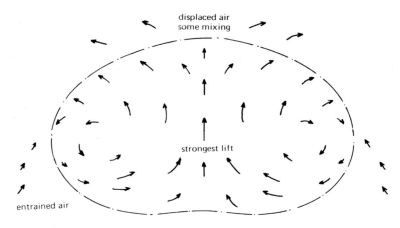

Figure 20. The structure of a thermal. The circulatory motion within the thermal gives a maximum velocity in the middle region of the core. Towards the top of the thermal the velocity slows down because the rising air is having to displace the air above. The entrained air around the side of the thermal will mostly be rising but after flying through it the glider will start to descend again as it enters the edge of the vortex ring. The first indications of rising air should therefore be ignored; however, if nothing better transpires it may be that the glider has been flown through the edge of the thermal (the entrained air that is) and not through the centre as the pilot might have hoped.

Finally, it must be emphasised that the selection of the right place under the cloud, usually the darkest part, and a positive approach to finding lift, is the only way to gain experience in cloud selection and improve one's ability to cloud read.

Early attempts at thermalling

First encounters with thermals are usually chance affairs; the thermal finds the glider rather than the pilot seeking out the lift. The aim, when local soaring, is generally to stay airborne as long as possible and it probably doesn't matter whether the glider is climbed efficiently, that is at the maximum rate possible. Indeed, the pilot is glad to be climbing at all and this state of mind is one of the factors which limit his eventual achievement and performance in cross-country terms (as evident by 'running-out-of-day' in attempts at 300 kilometres).

How can this be dealt with? To some extent the influence of

soaring-orientated instructors can set the student along the right lines by teaching him to soar in the first instance and encouraging an improved climb rate at all times. Only if the pilot adopts this philosophy will good performances be achieved.

This point is reinforced by analysing a 300-kilometre flight. Assuming that the glider being flown has a glide angle of 1 in 30, then to glide 300 kilometres requires a total height gain of 10 kilometres (further assumptions are that the task is a close circuit one and the wind can be ignored – that is its effects average out around the triangle – which is not necessarily true of course).

Distance 300 km requires 10 km height gain (33,000 ft approx.)

The number of thermals used will obviously depend upon the height band, which in turn is influenced by the cloud base and the lowest height that the pilot will be prepared to use regularly. A typical situation might be as shown in Figure 21, with the lower limit being determined by the ability of the pilot to pick up the next lift and his concern at landing in a field. The latter point may only be affected by the inconvenience of a retrieve – the Sunday evening syndrome – but this is often only an excuse to cover a genuine concern at the ability to land in a field.

Figure 21. *Using the best height band.* Realising that these alternatives are idealised, the local-soaring pilot will (a) aim to stay high and use the upper height band and every thermal, while the experienced cross-country pilot will (b) use the lower height band and the strongest lift as well as being able to select or reject the best thermals.

Some other factors which influence the height band used and the style of flying are:

1. The climb rate may well reduce near to cloud base, not neces-
    sarily because the lift is weaker but due to the difficulty in
    staying centred when the surges are not so marked as lower
    down. To some extent this may also be due to a lack of
    concentration or giving part of one's attention to navigational
    matters and looking for the next likely cloud.

2. The lower limit that a pilot sets himself depends on his
    confidence in soaring, his success at selecting the next source
    of lift and his reluctance or under-confidence to land out.
    Confidence will be boosted if the pilot considers how readily
    he contacts lift off a two-thousand-foot aerotow.

3. The local-soaring pilot is likely to have two closely associated
    handicaps; a desire to stay as high as possible and, to that end,
    to use every scrap of lift he encounters. His progress across
    country will, at best, be like that shown as (a) in Figure 21; it
    should be obvious that progress will be slow.

4. The pilot with confidence will use the lower height band which
    has the advantage of using the best lift and also seeing more
    easily where the next lift is because he does not climb to cloud
    base. The comparative figures in overall performance for each
    height band are:

Flight phase	Height band	
	5,000 to 4,000 ft	4,000 to 2,000 ft
Time to climb 33,000 ft	33 (thermals) × 5 min. = 165 min.	16·5 (thermals) × 5 min. = 82·5 min.
Time to centre in each thermal – say 4 turns of 30 sec. each	33 × 2 = 66 min.	16·5 × 2 = 33 min.
TOTAL	231 min.	115·5 min.

The assumption that on average the glider will be centred in the
thermal after four turns is probably a generous one, but whatever it
may be, the important point is that using the wrong height band will
as much as double the thermalling time.

Gliding between thermals should also be considered. Apart from
the advantages of not climbing to cloud base in terms of reading the
sky ahead and choosing a route along a line of clouds, it is likely that

the local-soaring pilot will not glide purposefully towards the next lift. Even assuming that both pilots in the example above glide at the same speed – say 100 kph* for ease of reckoning – then three hours of gliding added to the centring and climbing time brings the 'stay-high' pilot to a total flight time of nearly seven hours, which may well be longer than the soaring conditions last.

To highlight further the problems which the stay-high pilot faces, one should consider the number of times he may – probably does – persist with weak lift, lift which fails to live up to its initial promise, or in which he fails to centre. This will increase the time to climb still further.

Looking at it another way, if the glider is being flown between thermals at say 120 kph and the thermal-searching turn takes 30 seconds then:

Every circle flown is equivalent to one kilometre of distance lost or ground not covered. One hundred and twenty of these circles adds one hour to the flight.

Alternatively:

Every circle that can be dispensed with is a benefit in terms of distance flown and speed. What is required on the pilot's part is recognition of the need to fly straight as often as possible, and ignore or reject weak lift.

The cross-country flight looked at in these terms should emphasise the need for a style of thermal flying which may be summed up as follows:

1. Always strive to improve the climb rate, accepting of course that there will be a definite limit to it.
2. Establish as soon as possible the best height band, on the basis of the climb rate achieved at various heights, and use it. A proviso is, of course, that if the weather does not look good ahead then staying high may be essential.
3. Leave lift which has deteriorated if it cannot be re-centred in a turn or two, unless of course leaving it means falling down.
4. Any time lift is encountered in the glide, try to suppress the desire, which is perhaps already a habit, to circle in it unless it is particularly good – remember how much time will be lost in centring and how many kilometres are lost by circling.

* 100 kph = 54 kt

In terms of achieving your first 300-kilometre flight, techniques can be improved around much smaller tasks, but more of this later. If you recognise the handicaps and habits that it is so easy to acquire, you can set about remedying them or avoiding them now!

A positive approach to local soaring

One of the things that local soaring lacks is the extra stimulus or incentive that being out of gliding range of one's base airfield brings. Until you have a certain amount of experience it is unwise to venture too far away from the home airfield – generally you will not be allowed to do so anyway. It is a problem for instructors to impose realistic constraints – in terms of defining a local soaring area – to allow a solo pilot some freedom yet not expose him to risks with which he may be unable to cope. Poor airmanship in soaring is a common cause of accidents. To deal with this failing in the system requires a much more positive approach to soaring training which in return requires more instructors who have broad experience of soaring pilots. Some of the following suggestions and exercises are equally appropriate whether dual or solo.

First, however, a look at some of the more usual recommendations or rules which should constrain a pilot:

Don't circle below 500 ft.

Don't turn your back on the airfield below circuit height.

Don't go too far behind the downwind boundary.

These rules, sensibly interpreted, safeguard a pilot from drifting away from the airfield (downwind or in cross-winds) and from conflicting with other circuit traffic. The only rule which causes problems if adhered to too strictly is the second one. If there is a cross-wind drifting the glider towards the field (in the downwind-leg phase of the circuit) then it may often be better to make a turn away from the airfield rather than cramp the circuit.

However, despite these constraints, it is possible to climb away in lift from the circuit area without breaking the rules because once the glider is above circuit height it is generally accepted that it can be downwind of the airfield. The difficulty is in judging this or in laying down hard and fast rules to safeguard an early solo or local-soaring pilot. Ideally, of course, increasing confidence will encourage the pilot to range further from the field and with occasional exciting moments he will learn what rate of climb is required in a certain wind strength and the speed to fly for the best glide performance.

This knowledge must combine with decisiveness if the decision whether or not to land out is to be taken correctly. When a critical situation does arise a lack of knowledge together with indecisiveness could combine to cause an accident.

Having drifted downwind, the pilot decides to return to the airfield; what knowledge and disciplines will he need?

Assume for the moment that the glider can get back to the airfield, although the pilot may not believe it. If he is not sufficiently confident about landing out then he will almost certainly attempt to get back. The speed at which the glider is flown is of course critical – but does the pilot know what it is? The situation is complicated; not only is the wind to be taken into account but also the effects of rising and sinking air. The speed-to-fly ring takes into account the vertical motion of the atmosphere (see page 139). There should be one fitted. The effect of wind can be dealt with in two ways: either by using a final glide calculator or by rule of thumb. The former is certainly more accurate but least likely for an early solo pilot and the best advice will be based on an approximation of speed for best glide plus, say, half the wind speed (for a K8 this would be 42 kt plus 7 or 8 for a 15 kt wind, which is 50 kt). It is however increasingly my view that the final glide or local-soaring calculators should be carried and their use taught much earlier in a pilot's experience than has been the practice in the past. The reasoning behind this suggestion is that as glider performance improves it becomes increasingly difficult to 'eyeball' a glide; that is, to see whether the goal will be achieved. Judgement is difficult when the effect of wind and rising or sinking air have to be taken into account at the same time.

Imagine, as you probably can, this glide back to the airfield. The perception as to whether the airfield will be reached is difficult and may be impossible if the glide performance is in the order of 30:1. Even if the perception is possible, there is a need to 'average' the periods when the glider is flying through sink and going below the glide path (periods of despair) and when it is flying through lift and gaining on the glide path (periods of elation); this averaging is quite difficult to do. The assessment is made more difficult simply because the periods of despair always seem longer than the periods of elation. There is also the risk that the pilot will be quite frequently changing his decision as to whether to land out or not; this amounts to making no decision at all. The glide back may well be continued until any decision to go into a field is made too late for the approach into it to be an organised one.

The perception problems in this glide are, of course, the same as those in the approach. It is generally acknowledged however that many pilots are poor at recognising the potential undershoot for the simple reason that it is rarely demonstrated.

Under stress, the pilot may not be able to recognise whether the glide path required is being achieved. He may also fail to do two other things of importance; the first of these is to resist the temptation to increase the speed – to get the glide back over and done with. This is akin to driving a motor car at night with the only garage right at the limit of fuel range; to hold the speed down to forty or fifty miles per hour requires considerable restraint. The second thing that the pilot may fail to do is choose the best way back, in sky-reading terms. The direct route back may not pass under any cloud at all yet half a mile to one side is a line of cumulus. Of course, if the glider is very low, the cloud position may not be a good guide.

Overall, the problem relates to the wind, the glider's performance and flying at the correct speed, perception and decision making. Any pilot interested in improving his soaring skills would be well advised to study the fields in the local area as well as gain the knowledge to fly his glider properly. The relevant areas of knowledge will be dealt with separately later.

It might prove of practical value to have a pilot carry a local area map marked up at various distances both upwind and downwind, with the height required to get back to the airfield at circuit-starting height – say a thousand feet to be on the safe side. Figure 22 shows a simple map with suitable markings for a 15-knot wind, and is based on the performance of a K8 glider.

A glide calculator enables the pilot to work out quickly the height needed for a given distance (or the distance the glider will travel from a given height) taking into account the wind; it also gives the pilot the speed to fly for the wind component. The calculator shown in Figures 14b and 23 is known as the JSW local soaring calculator because it was designed by J. S. Williamson, twice British National Champion, who has flown several times in World Championships.

At (a) – set for a 10-knot tail-wind component:

2,000 ft gives approximately 9·7 nm

3,000 ft gives approximately 14·6 nm

and the speed to fly is thirty-eight knots.

At (b) – set for a 20-knot head-wind component:
   2,000 ft gives approximately 4·0 nm
   3,000 ft gives approximately 6·1 nm
and the speed to fly is fifty knots.

With very little practice, these figures can be determined while flying, and the distance to go can be measured from the map. It will be best to use the quarter-million map (see page 74) for this purpose as it has more detail and will enable a more accurate pin-point than would be possible with the half-million map. The calculator, it should be noted, has scales down both sides so that distances can be measured off the map.

The second requirement to increase safety in local soaring is to recognise the risk of landing out. Ideally, one or two suitable fields downwind of the airfield for each wind direction should be identified so eliminating the selection part of the task. Once the decision has been made to go into the field, the only points to emphasise are orientation of the circuit and not 'crowding' it and any approach considerations such as turbulence in the lee of trees or undulating ground, as well as the perception problems and speed control requirements if an uphill landing is being made.

If practice approaches into the field are not possible, using a motor glider, say, then it would be helpful to visit the fields in question. If a group of solo pilots are accompanied by an instructor

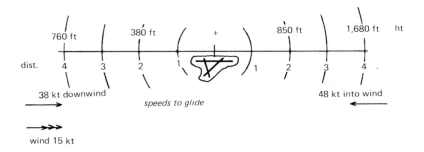

Figure 22. Gliding range (height v. distance) values.
With this information, which can be worked out in a few moments before the flight, the pilot is safeguarded from getting out of gliding range. It is not necessary to work out the height for each mile; more usefully it can be computed for local ground features or land marks; a margin for circuit height – one thousand feet – can be added.

then discussion may establish whether the students are confident or not. Although dealing with students in this way might just encourage an occasional landing-out that was not necessary, if it safeguards the less confident pilot, then it will have done much to make local soaring safer.

Field landings are dealt with elsewhere in this book (see Chapter 5) but it is important to mention the variation in the state of fields with the season and that at certain times out landings are unacceptable (e.g. in areas of extensive cereal crops, there may be no landable fields at all).

A typical local soaring accident will emphasise the importance of these various points which a pilot needs to learn or, for preference, be taught.

'I was launched in a K13 to attempt a thirty-minute soaring flight, after having been briefed regarding both thermal and wind strength.

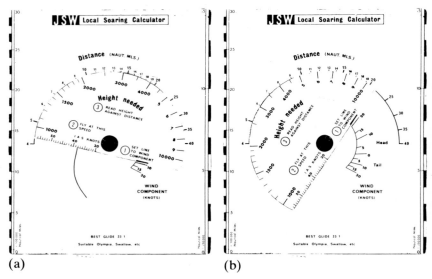

(a)   (b)

Figure 23. The local-soaring calculator.
The calculator at (a) is set for a 10-knot tail-wind and at (b) for a 20-knot head-wind.
The sequence of operation is:
1.   set the line to the wind component;
2.   read off the speed to fly from the lower left-hand scale where it intersects the curved line;
3.   read off height against distance from the outer curved scales.

On releasing at the top of the launch (autotow) I immediately contacted lift and commenced to soar. After twenty minutes, I realised that I was drifting away from the airfield and headed back. On leaving the last thermal at 1400 ft, I thought I had ample height to reach the airfield but when I was about three-quarters of a mile from the runway, I encountered up to six knots of sink and lost height quickly. When approximately four hundred yards from the airfield, with some construction works directly ahead of me, I realised that I would not be able to reach it so turned 90° cross-wind over a row of tall trees. My intention was to land across the field heading for the far corner. When heading into the field, the cross wind caused considerable drift and although I attempted to correct the drift, it caused me to collide with a tree.'*

The glider was still airborne when it hit the tree, which was one hundred and fifty yards into the field. The field was one hundred and seventy-five yards long. With an approach over tall trees, landing in the field was probably impossible!

* First published in *Sailplane and Gliding Magazine* June/July 1975, in an article entitled 'Accident Review – The Cost of Indecision'.

3   Improving the Cross-country Skills

The experience gained in local soaring is of limited value in progress towards cross-country flying unless a pilot – one hopes helped by his instructors – identifies the areas in which his skills must be developed.

The exercises detailed in Chapter 2 (Purpose for Every Flight) were specifically designed to make use of non-soarable days; in the same way a much more positive approach can be taken towards local soaring to develop cross-country skills. Taking one point from the last chapter – 'every circle flown is equivalent to one kilometre of distance lost or ground not covered' – it has been recognised in recent years that a glider can be soared in thermals without circling. This development, known as 'dolphin' soaring, has come about because of the improvement in glider performance. Having been developed as a technique it is now widely recognised as suitable for use in gliders which, it used to be thought, did not have the performance to soar in this way.

To give you an appreciation of this concept, the barograph trace shown below (Figure 24) was a 300-kilometre flight at a speed better than 100 k.p.h. in which the glider was not circled for the last two hours.

Contrast this with the local-soaring pilot who, whenever he finds lift, circles in it. By the time this pilot soars across country, it has become a reflex action to circle when the variometer indicates rising air. So much so that many pilots, even when final gliding, are unable to resist the temptation to make a turn or two in good lift. The consequence of course is that they arrive back at the airfield with several hundred feet to spare. The cross-country pilot who wants to make real progress should be able to decide whether it is best to circle or dolphin. The first requirement is to suppress the circling reflex, and a local soaring flight can be organised to aid this.

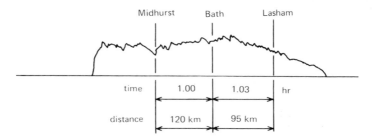

Figure 24. Barograph trace – 2 hours without circling.
Although the glider was a Nimbus 2 with a best glide angle approaching 1 in 50, it does stretch the imagination rather to conceive of two hours' flying in a glider without circling. Even assuming a glide angle of 1 in 40, the height requirement for a 200-kilometre glide is 5 kilometres or 16,400 feet, so that the lift used while flying straight and pulling up or S-turning has provided the equivalent input in energy terms.

Using the first thermal off tow, climb to within five hundred feet of cloud base (any higher obscures the view of the sky ahead). Select the best-looking section of sky in a substantially upwind direction, and see how far the glider can be flown without circling. Either pull up (i.e. reduce speed) or S-turn if the lift is particularly good. Have a map of the local area marked up with height/distance lines, rather than calculate the figure in the air (although with a little practice the calculation is not difficult). Progressively reduce the margins in the glide back to the airfield arriving first at a position to join the circuit at twelve hundred feet or so, later reducing this to circuit height or even a little less as confidence in the glider's performance increases.

Tiny triangles
The concept of 'tiny triangles' makes a local flight much more purposeful and, perhaps more importantly, means that the style of flying is similar to that on longer cross-countries. The only difference is that you are not out of gliding range of an airfield – in this case your home airfield – which means that the stress is reduced.
     The size of the triangle is not critical, but should take into account the conditions (strength of lift and height of cloud base), the performance of the glider and the wind. If the wind is moderate, then it may be desirable to have two turning points upwind, and the airfield as the third one; alternatively, three turning points around the airfield can be used. The turning point should be easily recognisable

by 'pinpoint' features – not whole towns or whole airfields, but a tall building in the town or an airfield control tower; road junctions, churches, ponds (if they are not too large) are all equally good.

It will help if you have identified the chosen points in previous flights or go off specifically to have a look. One important aspect is that if the turning points are to be photographed – and this is good practice if you aspire to a Gold 'C'. The sector in which the photograph is to be taken must be identified in relation to features on the ground; many a claim for a 300-kilometre flight has been rejected because of incorrect turning-point evidence, so why not practise in the local area? The photography can even be practised on non-soarable days by taking pictures of suitable points on the ground, obviously taking care not to conflict with circuit traffic. Use imaginary track lines into and away from the feature. Turning-point photography will be dealt with in more detail later. (See Appendix 3.)

Having established the turning points and made sure of them, without any more ado set off around the triangle. If it is twenty kilometres or so, then it might take half an hour to get round. If you find yourself using all the lift available – circling in every thermal – then you are probably failing to use the glider's performance. Realise that a glider with a best glide angle of 1 in 25 needs only 1,000 metres of height (3,280 ft) to cover 25 kilometres. Given that, one climb to 4,500 ft would let you glide round without circling again, provided the lift and sinking air averaged out.

When you become bored with this basic exercise, take the next step in the list below:

1. Know your local area well enough to be sure that you can identify the turning point easily.
2. Go round the triangle once using lift as you see fit and note the time taken. If the speed is particularly slow or fast go round a second or third time and take the average.
3. If you can get sufficient height, go around without circling at all, but fly the speed-to-fly ring; since you are within gliding range of your airfield, you can always land back if you run short of height.
4. Once you are convinced of the height necessary to go around, go round a further time but this time use only the best lift. This should improve the speed considerably.

Once you have got speed up to fifty or sixty kilometres per hour, Gold 'C' distance becomes a possibility, as long as you can navigate.

Progress to Gold 'C' distance and Diamond goal.

Broadening of experience towards completion of the Gold badge should be done progressively. One of the particular problems regarding the 300-kilometre flight is that many pilots are teaching themselves to navigate as they do it, and getting lost may well be the cause of failure. At the same time as improving soaring performance, one can progressively get to know the countryside by a series of tasks all related to the probable or possible Gold 'C' task.

By setting out-and-returns or 'flat' triangles along the first and last legs of the 300-kilometre triangle task, the navigational problem will be largely overcome, putting the pilot over familiar terrain except in the middle leg of the triangle. Suitable tasks might be as shown in Figure 25.

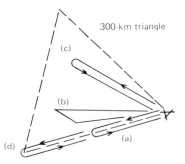

Figure 25. Training tasks for the 300-kilometre triangle.
The flights shown may also be made along the third leg:
(a)   100 km out-and-return (i.e. 50 km out and 50 km back).
(b)   A flat triangle going towards the centre of the second leg (of the 300-km triangle).
(c)   Out-and-return towards the second turning point.
(d)   Out-and-return to first turning point.
    Some or all of the tasks might be repeated along the third leg and so, when the 300-km triangle is eventually attempted, the pilot will have much less difficulty with navigation.

Improving soaring performance — analysis of barograph traces

The motivation to improve one's performance in soaring terms must come from within. Performance however is not easily gauged except in competition. Outside competitions, one of the ways in which a comparison performance can be gained is to look at the barograph traces – comparing yours against that of a more experienced pilot. After a little practice, it is not difficult to see the mistakes that have been made. All too often the impressions one is left with after a flight are totally subjective; 'I spent hours scratching at eight hundred feet' (probably twenty minutes); 'then there was this fantastic six-knot thermal' (the barograph trace shows three). Or 'I only used ten thermals for the whole of the task.' And so it goes on.

A detailed analysis reveals the truth and gives more positive direction to improvements on the next flight. The figure below, Figure 26, gives calibrated rates of climb for a standard barograph* and this can be used to determine actual climb rates.

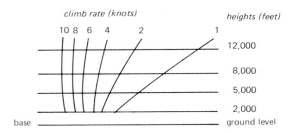

Figure 26. Barograph trace interpretation.

(a)   Each of the climbs is through the height range from 2,000 to 12,000 feet. Using this calibration reproduced on transparent film, it can be laid over the barograph trace to be analysed.

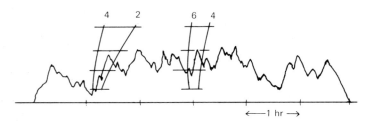

(b)   This is done in barograph trace from a 300-kilometre flight.

---

* Winter 10 km/10 hr rotation rate.

This trace shows a number of interesting features;

1. Frequently the climb rate reduces towards the top of the thermals; it is not all that obvious, but careful scrutiny and a comparison with the calibration shows this point.

2. The height band used was 9,000 to 13,500 ft* in the middle phase of the flight (apart from one low point near the second turning point). However, there is a marked tendency to stop and use lift after very little height has been lost. Rarely was the rate of climb as good as the longer climb started lower down.

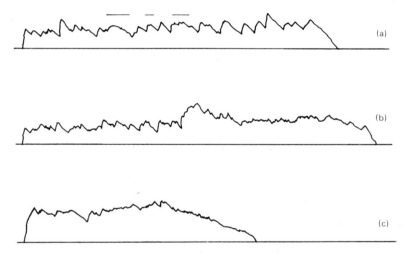

Figure 27. More barograph traces.
These traces show a number of interesting features:
(a) This trace is reminiscent of the 'saw-tooth' variety but shows a certain amount of 'dolphin-flying' – that is pulling up in the lift but not stopping to circle – these phases are marked. This flight was an out-and-return from Lasham to Exeter and back, a distance of 225 miles.
(b) A marked increase in dolphin-flying is apparent in this trace – the higher section in the middle of the flight was in wave.
(c) This trace looks more like a duration flight on a ridge with the lift getting weaker towards the end of the flight. In fact it was an undeclared 300-kilometre flight. The glider was not circled during the last 230 km, which distance was covered in two hours and ten minutes.

---

* and terrain height 4600 – 5000 ft.

3.   The time to get centred was often considerable (the sub-scale on the diagram below the base line shows the time scale); contrast the sharp transitions from descent to climb with the others.

'My recollections of the flight [Fig. 26b still] are vague but one point stands out clearly: I was quite pleased with progress around the second leg which, despite the fact that the wrong road was followed out of the first turning point, seemed to go well. However, on comparing notes with another pilot it transpired that he hadn't stopped to circle at all along this leg, and that in a 15-metre glider – mine was a Kestrel 19.'

This should only serve to reinforce the need to suppress the desire to circle every time lift is encountered. Indeed, this next comparison of a classic barograph trace of the 'saw-tooth' variety with the present day dolphin-flying sorts shows in sharp contrast the changes in technique that have occurred in recent years.

A well-kept logbook with barograph traces for all flights will show whether one's technique has changed and any shortcomings in it. In terms of analysing soaring and cross-country flights, the barograph is an under-rated instrument.

4 Navigation

For the glider pilot, formal navigational training will at best consist
of some map reading practice in a two-seater – usually a motor
glider. The fundamental problem in navigating a glider is that the
often irregular progress that one makes (compared to aeroplanes)
when flying across country does not lend itself to a computation
based on speed, direction and wind. Speed variation is dependent
not only upon the proportion of time spent circling and gliding, but
also on changes in the weather, for better or worse. Direction too
will vary as the need arises to skirt areas of cloud shadow or poor
thermal-producing terrain, or to go around controlled airspace.
Finally, the effect of wind must be allowed for. Since the speed and
direction do not, as a rule, remain constant, it is not possible to
compute, before take-off, the average or approximate effects of the
wind. Most pilots become aware of the wind only when they are
unable to progress against it or cannot maintain a desired track
(path over the ground) when the wind is across that track. When its
effects are not as obvious as this, a pilot may become confused
because the next feature fails to appear where he expects it or
appears sooner than expected. Once there is some confusion
about the glider's position then the pilot's mind starts to play tricks
on him.

What then is the solution to learning how to navigate? How does
a pilot without experience of cross-country flying get to the stage of
knowing where he is the whole of the time? I think the key to the
problem is work-load. It has been suggested before in this book that
a balanced work-load is achieved only when the various cross-
country skills are developed. A pilot who frequently gets low –
down to field-selection height – and is worried about landings out
will become totally preoccupied with the out-landing and almost
certainly pay little attention to soaring prospects. In this situation,

navigation will get none of his attention. Even when the pilot can soar consistently, the prospect of landing may still demand a lot of attention, so that map reading is neglected. The choice of the words 'map reading' is deliberate because this is the most important part of the business.

Map reading

Perhaps the most important point to appreciate from the outset is that it is very difficult to use a map while the glider is being circled. Only when flying straight is it possible to get orientated and relate the features on the ground to the pictorial presentation of them on the map. Here is the first problem; the map representation of a ground feature should conjure up a picture in the pilot's mind. Often it does not, and this is because pilot may not be familiar enough with the symbols. This is borne out in poring over maps with instructors while planning cross-country flights – 'tell me what features you would use on this flight' and they will pick out the features which are prominent on the map but not necessarily obvious on the ground. First you must become thoroughly familiar with the map symbols so that you can relate the view from the cockpit with the pictures on the map.

The first decision to make is what sort of maps to use. The choice is limited. There are two scales of map (more usually termed charts); the half-million and the quarter-million. The scale of a map is expressed as a ratio, so the half-million map has a scale of 1:500,000. This means that one unit of distance on the map is equivalent to half a million of the same units on the ground. A pilot can choose to work in kilometres, nautical miles or statute miles, as he wishes. Expressed more conveniently, the half-million map can be converted to any of these three units from the scales at the bottom of the map.

To work out the scale of the map in miles per inch, all that is necessary is to divide the figure of half a million by the number of inches in a mile:

$$\text{One statute mile} = 5280 \text{ ft} = 63,360 \text{ inches}$$
$$\text{One nautical mile} = 6080 \text{ ft} = 72,960 \text{ inches}$$

So:

$$\text{One inch (on the map)} = 500,000/63,360 = 7 \cdot 9 \text{ st miles}$$
$$= 500,000/72,960 = 6 \cdot 85 \text{ nm.}$$

The choice of units perhaps warrants an explanation. Glider pilots tend to record the distance of their tasks in kilometres because the International badge requirements use these units. However, because speed (in most countries) is measured in knots (nautical miles per hour), it is logical to use the same units for distance. The origin of the nautical mile is straightforward and the logic of it will become apparent from the following.

Any two points on the earth's surface may be related one to another in terms of their longitude and latitude, Latitude is measured in degrees of arc between the equator (0°) and the poles (90°N or 90°S). A division of one degree is sub-divided into minutes of arc, and sixty minutes equal one degree.

One minute of arc equals one nautical mile (6080 ft) and this is the connection. It is of practical value in that the distance can be taken directly from the latitude grid on the map. For example: 52°N to 53°N (1° = sixty minutes of arc) = 60 nm.

Do not be misled into thinking that the vertical grid lines measuring longitude have the same relationship to distance. Longitude is a measure of a given point's distance from the Greenwich Meridian; the distance between the Greenwich Meridian and the next one to the west – 1° W, or between any others, varies from the equator to the pole as the lines converge to the poles and cannot be used as a measure of distance (see Figure 31).

I have neglected here to go into the methods of map projection. The map represents the curved surface of the earth on a flat surface, so some distortion is inevitable. On conventional aviation maps, lines of latitude (horizontal) curve slightly, the ends of the arc being higher than the middle (in the Northern Hemisphere), and lines of longitude (vertical) converge slightly towards the top of the map (in the Northern Hemisphere). This type of projection is known as the Lambert's Conformal. If you want further details of map projections and characteristics, then any good text book on navigation will give them.

Having digressed to these fundamentals, it still remains to make the choice of map. Most inexperienced pilots, when faced with the two scales, half- and quarter-million, will probably choose the latter for the simple reason that it looks more like the conventional road map. It has, however, one disadvantage, that roads predominate. This may lead you to rely on them as navigational features more than you should. The disadvantages of the quarter-million map are:

1. Too much detail may encourage too much attention to navigation.
2. The large scale may mean that too many separate maps have to be used for a long flight.
3. Only controlled airspace at or below 3,000 ft AMSL* is shown; if you fly higher than that you need the half-million chart as well. Alternatively, you can mark up the quarter-million map yourself.
4. The use of colour to indicate relief – the shading between the height contours – 'clutters' the map.

Contrast this with the half-million map, which seems to have insufficient detail in some cases; for example, some towns are marked but not named, and motorways and dual-carriageways are represented by the same symbol.

The best compromise is to use the map which suits you best or most suits the occasion. Many experienced pilots will use the quarter-million map for the detailed navigation at turning points and the half-million map for en route between them. Only practice in the use of each scale will familiarise you with its advantages or shortcomings.

Next, it is appropriate to consider the various features which are always given at the foot of the map; commonly called the legend; the fashionable word is now 'culture'. Figure 28 below compares the two. Also at the foot is the date when the map was last revised. This is important on two counts: airspace information may change, and recently constructed features may not be incorporated (e.g. reservoirs, pylons, motorways, etc.).

There are a number of considerations regarding the features on the ground, looking for them, the ease with which they can be seen etc., and it is worth bearing these points in mind when considering any feature. These factors are:

Visibility
For early cross-country flights the visibility should be good. In navigating from feature to feature there is a tendency to search for the next one at the limit of visibility – in other words on the horizon.

* AMSL: Above Mean Sea Level

(a)

(b)

Figure 28. Map legends or cultures for the half- and quarter-million maps.
(a) Quarter-million (b) Half-million.

It may be that the feature is not that far away and in looking beyond it you may fail to see it. Pilots get lost in good visibility as well as bad. To look in the right place, it is useful to know how far away the feature is. If the visibility is ten miles and the feature you are looking for five or so miles away, do not look to the limits of visibility.

The nature of the feature
Towns, moderate expanses of water and some airfields may be visible from a distance of several miles. An early sighting will often attract you towards the feature, possibility losing your sense of direction and sense of time. With a better view from close to, it may not prove to be what you thought.

Line features, motorways and railways in particular, may not be visible until a mile or two away. An awareness of this fact is essential if one is not to become anxious about fixing position.

Obscuring factors
Bad visibility apart, good features may be obscured by the lie of the land (a town at the foot of an escarpment for example), or by cloud shadow. Airfields are notorious for the way they can be concealed by cloud shadow.

Features on maps

Roads
There are a variety of symbols to indicate the different categories of road, especially on the quarter-million map (refer to Figure 28). It is important to appreciate a number of disadvantages:

1. The width of a road is not to scale on the map, and so roads are not as prominent as they are shown.
2. Too many roads are marked on the quarter-million map, so it is easy to become confused.
3. Even the identifying feature of 'bridges over' motorways (rather than conventional road junctions) may not be enough to differentiate between motorways and dual carriageways. It is important not to become confused.
4. Unless your track lies along or adjacent to an easily identifiable road, a road may serve only as a distance fix – showing how far you are along the track. Additional features will be necessary to show whether you are on track or not. The angle

at which the road (or any other line feature) is crossed is a useful cross-check but this must be confirmed against compass reading, and allowance made for drift corrections.

Some roads, however, are very good features; these include Roman roads (easily identified by their straightness), and motorways and some road junctions which are recognised for their individual layout.

Railways
These have always been regarded as good features, and a pilot may often resort to following one towards a particular town. This is all very well if there is only one line in, but may lead to the mistake of following another line out of the town. Beware, if there is more than one line; cross-check that it is the right one by the compass reading.

The gradual disappearance of all but main line railways has reduced their usefulness to some extent. The quarter-million map discriminates between those in use, disused and dismantled (also narrow gauge) but the half-million map no longer makes such distinction. So using one map requires you to ignore the track of a railway on the ground; using the other does not.

Supplementary features such as stations, level crossings and tunnels are all shown on the quarter-million, but only tunnels appear on the half-million.

Towns
One of the principal problems of a town is getting an appreciation of its size from the map if you do not know it already. Although the outline shape of the larger towns is shown on both maps, it is still quite easy to be misled. Bearing in mind that the scale of one map is twice that of the other, one may have the impression of a size of a town which in itself is wrong. To make the impression less subjective, it may help to work out an included angle of a certain size of town say four miles across – when seen from a certain distance. This is thirty degrees from eight miles and twenty degrees from twelve miles.

It is also essential to check the town by other features in it or around, no matter how certain you are that it is the town you expected. The pattern of roads, railways, rivers, canals and cathedrals is usually quite distinctive. Confusion may arise over large villages – recently developed perhaps – shown on the quarter-million but not appearing at all on the half-million map.

Water

Lakes, reservoirs, rivers and canals often stand out well, especially so if the sun is shining on them. It should be recognised that in some parts, where waterways proliferate, it is easy to be confused. Also there may be little resemblance between the ground and the map if there has been recent flooding. The only real problem that arises concerns small lakes, which may not appear on the half-million map. The coast line, even when seen from a distance, is usually quite distinctive; the only problem is that if you get too near it, you may be unable to soar.

Other natural features

Woods or forests and hills are often distinctive, and may serve to give a 'fix' (an exact identification of position). Clearly identifiable too are ranges of hills, but if they aren't very high and are very irregular in shape, they should not be relied on for an accurate fix, unless backed up by another feature. Some woods are distinctive in their shape, but a small wood in generally wooded terrain should not be relied on.

Other man-made features

These include radio or television masts and high-tension and electricity systems – the sort on pylons; the latter are shown only on the quarter-million map but often help confirm a position. Masts may not be too easy to see in some circumstances – when passed over close to and in cloud shadow for instance. They may be easy to see if you are lower than the top of them, but then you are probably pre-occupied with other things.

Airfields

Last but not least in significance come airfields, which range from active ones with their own controlled airspace to fields which have been disused for many years. For navigational purposes, airfields are rather like towns. They should be checked out by other adjacent distinguishing features. Unlike towns, they may be in open country with nothing to identify them, and if this is the case they should not be relied on. In some places there are a lot of airfields which may be distinctive as a group, but even then they should be checked carefully with regard to their orientation to the glider's track. Cloud shadow has already been mentioned as a factor which may camouflage ground features; this is particularly true of airfields.

There are some basics of navigation which an aeroplane pilot learns as a matter of course; the glider pilot may have to teach himself, occasionally from bitter experience. Use of the compass is seldom taught, with the result that pilots are frequently less well orientated than they need be.

The magnetic compass

There are a number of fundamental problems in making an instrument respond to the earth's magnetic field. In recent developments – notably the Bohli compass – most have been overcome, but since most compasses in gliders are basic, that type must be dealt with first.

The basic principle of a compass is that a freely suspended magnet will align itself with the earth's magnetic field, its North-seeking end pointing towards the North magnetic pole. The first thing that is evident in a basic system is that the North-seeking end of the magnet points downwards at an angle to the horizontal (unless it is at the earth's magnetic equator); this angle is termed the angle of dip and causes some problems in the design and use of the instrument. So that the magnetic system lies horizontally – only if it does can it be related to the compass card – it is suspended by a pivot placed above its centre of gravity so that the mass hangs below the pivot and largely overcomes the dip effect. This creates two side effects. The first of these is called acceleration error.

Acceleration errors

These errors are at their worse when a glider is being flown either West or East and give the following faults (in the Northern Hemisphere).

If the speed of the glider is increased, then the compass indicates an apparent turn to the North even though the glider is not actually turning. The amount of this apparent turn depends on the acceleration – the more it is, the greater the indicated turn. If the speed is allowed to settle, then the compass will indicate the original heading after a few seconds.

The reverse is true of deceleration.

This error is not evident at all on Northerly or Southerly headings and reduces progressively from West or East to North and South; Figure 29 illustrates this:

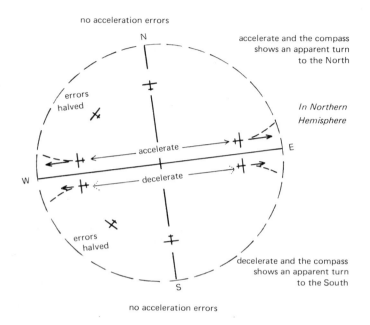

Figure 29. The compass: acceleration errors. The errors – apparent turns – are shown if a glider is flown in the various directions. If this is too much to remember, as it might be when trying to straighten up in a cloud, then just remember to 'ignore the compass when heading West or East if the glider's speed is changing'.

The second set of errors show up when the glider is turning.

Turning errors

As anyone knows who has tried to straighten up on a heading in order to come out of cloud the compass seems to be a diabolical invention. Before it can be used to straighten up on to a heading, its faults must be understood.

First of all the compass can only keep pace with the glider if the turns are gentle – probably at no more than ten degrees of bank; moreover, it may take two or three such turns – after turning more steeply – for the compass to settle down. The errors are best explored by flying straight and then starting a gentle turn in the following way.

1. With the glider heading North, start a gentle turn to the left i.e. to the West; as the turn is commenced the compass will be reluctant to move and may even indicate a turn to the right. Ignore this, however, and after turning through 20° or 30° the compass will indicate a turn towards the West. Level the glider's wings 5° or 10° before the compass indicates West, and the compass will settle on a Westerly heading. There are no turning errors on a Westerly heading.

2. Turn left again; as the glider's nose comes around to the South, the compass will show a quickening rate of turn; it will indicate South before the glider is pointing in that direction. When the compass has gone 30° past South,* level the wings and the compass will swing back to settle on a Southerly indication.

3. Turning left again the compass will be lively and a quicker turn than is actually being made will be indicated. To straighten in an Easterly direction, the same allowance as in (1) should be made – straighten 5° or 10° before the compass indicates East.

4. Finally, turn left once more to straighten on a Northerly heading; the glider's wings should be levelled 30° before the Northerly heading is indicated on the instrument.

So far all headings used have been cardinal ones of North, South, East and West. It is more usual in flying and gliding to talk in terms of degrees: 360° (N), 180° (S), 090° (E) and 270° (W). Note that North is also 000°, but 360° is the more usual. Get used to thinking in terms of degrees rather than cardinal headings because measurements from the map will be directly in degrees. The next figure, Figure 30, shows the turning errors.

To straighten on to intermediate headings, 315° (NW), 225° (SW), 135° (SE) and 045° (NE), the allowance for turning error should be halved: in the Southern sector, 15° more than appears necessary and in the Northern sector 15° less (as indicated by the compass).

---

* Thirty degrees is an approximate allowance and will vary from one instrument to another; it may also vary slightly with the rate of turn.

Again, if this is too much remember, then always straighten on Westerly or Easterly headings.

These errors, it should be noted, would be reversed in the Southern Hemisphere; like the acceleration errors any explanation of the dynamics would only serve to complicate the issue.

The sum of compass errors together may baffle even quite an experienced pilot, but with a little practice (on non-soaring days) the instrument can become a useful aid to cross-country flying, especially when needed to straighten up on track with no ground features to help orientation. In this respect, it is worth mentioning another reliable aid – namely the sun – which lies to the South (in the Northern Hemisphere) at noon (Greenwich Mean Time, GMT) or at 1300 hr (British Summer Time, BST) and moves around at 15° per hour.

In addition to the use of the compass in flight, there are flight-planning considerations which have to be understood if the in-flight use of the instrument is to be of any value.

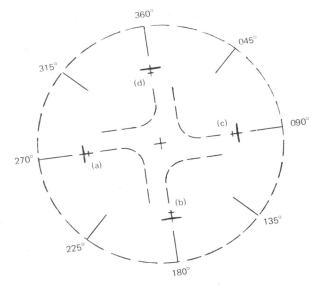

Figure 30. Correcting for turning errors. (a). Straighten when the compass shows 280 or 275° (for West). (b) Straighten when the compass shows 150° (for South). (c) Straighten when the compass shows 100 or 095° (for East). (d) Straighten when the compass shows 030° (for North).
Note: all turns to the left

Flight planning considerations

In this context we are concerned with converting the angular measurements of the proposed track of the flight with regard to the
meridian (a line running from North to South along the earth's
surface). The map grid and the proposed track of a flight are shown
in Figure 31.

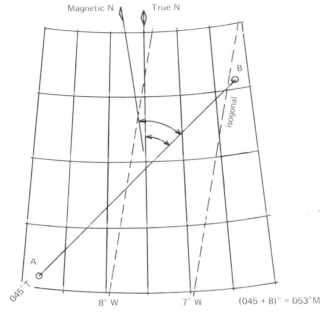

Figure 31. The map grid. The curvature of the horizontal lines and the
convergence of the vertical ones are exaggerated (see page 75). The flight
to be made in the direction A to B is measured from the meridian (strictly at
mid-track) and is 45° (045° is the correct way of expessing it) and this is the
true track (Tr. (T): Track True).

Making this angular measurement at mid-track is only relevant to
very long flights and a detailed explanation needs a deeper understanding of map projection and navigational theory than this book
warrants.*

The first correction to be made to this figure (045°) is to correct it
for variations in the earth's magnetic field. This correction is given
on the map.

* See Bibliography.

There are lines joining together places of equal magnetic variation; for the UK the figures range from 11° W in Ireland to 7° W in South-East England. The 'West' means that the magnetic North pole lies to the West of the true meridian. Note that the line joining places of equal magnetic variation – known as an isogonal – is not a 'magnetic meridian'.

To convert the true track to a magnetic track, variation must be added if it is West (W) or subtracted if it is East (E). If the variation is 9° West, then the magnetic track (Tr. (M)) is:

$$045° + 8° = 053° \text{ M.}$$

There's an old saw, 'variation West, compass best; variation East, compass least,' which aims to help you remember to add or subtract the variation accordingly.

It is probably easier however to visualise where magnetic North lies in relation to the true meridian.

The final correction to make takes into account errors in the compass itself (due to the proximity of the metal of the aircraft). These errors are determined by a process known as 'swinging the compass' which, by a series of adjustments, reduces the errors to a minimum, any remaining errors being recorded. The errors are then placarded in the cockpit so that the pilot can correct the magnetic track (Tr. (M)) to a compass track (Tr. (C)). As the errors may be presented in one of three different ways, these are shown in Figure 32.

To Fly	Steer	Or Correction	Or Deviation
N	000	0	0
045	047	+ 2	2° W
090	092	+ 2	2° W
135	134	− 1	1° E
180	177	− 3	3° E
225	223	− 2	2° E
270	270	0	0
315	316	+ 1	1° W

Figure 32. Presentation of Compass Errors.

By far the simplest presentation is the plus or minus correction; it saves the bother of remembering that W means add and E means subtract. Just occasionally, the correction is presented in a graphical form; the advantage of this is that intermediate readings can be interpolated.

In gliding if the compass has been swung and the errors minimised, they may be ignored for all practical purposes. Understanding of the instrument however would be incomplete without this knowledge.

To complete the example, using the figures in the table above, the compass course (strictly the compass track) would become:

$$053° + 2° = 055° \text{ (C)}$$

If a series of tracks are to be used on one flight, figures will usually be worked out in tabular form.

° C	DEV.	° M.	Var.	° T.
055	+ 2	053	8W	045

The headings to the columns, CDMVT, have various 'jingles' to help one remember the order. Cadbury's Dairy Milk Very Tasty is one of the more common (and repeatable), even if not the most memorable.

The next phase of planning a flight is to take into account the wind.

The effects of the wind

An aeroplane's or glider's track over the ground, and its ground speed, are modified by the wind, and despite the fact that a gliding cross-country is not flight planned in the way that an aeroplane flight is, still it may be of more than academic interest to look at the method of wind-allowance calculation. Aeroplane pilots disappear in the corner of the briefing room with mysterious-looking computers or calculators.

The effect of a NW wind (315°) on the track of an aircraft going from A to B (090° T) for example, is to drift it to the right of track. The pilot must correct for this if the desired track is to be maintained. The basis of the calculation is shown in Figure 33.

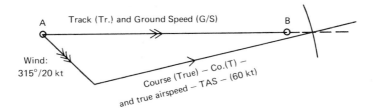

Figure 33. The vector triangle.

(a)   Draw a line in the direction of the wind to the downwind side of A. The length of the line will be the wind strength to some suitable scale – say 1 inch to 20 knots. Mark the line with three arrows to indicate that it represents the wind vector.

(b)   With a compass or divider set to represent the airspeed (strictly TAS), and with the point on the end of the wind vector, describe an arc to cut the track line. Join this point to the end of the wind vector with a line (which should be marked with one arrow); this represents the true course (Co. (T)) and the airspeed. The original line from A to B represents the track, and its length the ground speed. Co. (T) is 077° and the TAS 60 kt; ground speed (G/S) is 73 kt.

There are four known factors (it is not possible with less information) which enable you to compute the other two. It is a point worth noting that the wind speed is given in degrees (true) and is the direction from which the wind is blowing.

This calculation might seem irrelevant in a gliding context, but we will see shortly where it might be appropriate. Before doing so there is another 'rule of thumb' worth learning; it is known as 'the one-in-sixty rule'; the basis of it is shown in Figure 34.

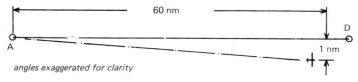

Figure 34. The one-in-sixty rule.

(a)   The required track is from A to D; if after 60 miles the glider is 1 mile off track, the angular error is 1 degree. This is not an absolutely accurate rule, but it serves as a good approximation.

A more realistic situation would be as shown below; where after thirty miles the aircraft is three miles off track.

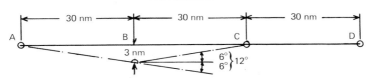

(b)   This area corresponds to 6 miles in 60 and is equivalent to 6°; the first adjustment that could be made is to alter course 6° to the left and fly parallel to track. Alternatively, the original track could be made good after another thirty miles by an initial alteration of 12° (left at B) and another alteration of 6° (right at C).

Yet another alternative, and perhaps the best, is to fly directly from B to D and the course alteration in this case would be:

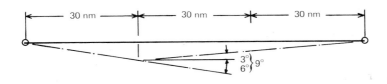

(c)   6° + 3° = 9° to the left.

In gliding this rule may be useful for starting a long final glide from a position somewhat off track.

Nowadays, the complexity of controlled airspace in some areas may make it essential to stay on track; also from some sites it is rarely possible to fly the 'traditional' downwind Silver 'C' distance of fifty kilometres.

Flying a cross-wind track in a glider may present a problem because whilst the glider is circling it is drifting and the track must be made good during the glide. The drift-correction triangle can only be solved if it is known how much time will be spent circling and cruising. The track over the ground would be as shown in Figure 35(a).

The other flight planning worth doing is to see the effect of wind on 300-kilometre triangle. Assume that without wind the task could be completed at 60 kilometres an hour (kph is usually used to express cross-country speeds). See Figure 36.

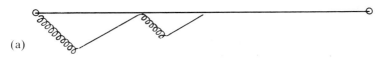

(a)

Figure 35. A cross-wind cross-country: allowance for drift.

The first approximation would be to assume that half the time would be spent circling and the remainder cruising (a), if the speed between thermals (A and D) were 50 kt and the wind was at 315°, then two vector triangles would have to be drawn. Assuming the circling to be continuous, the glider would drift from A to B (b). To glide from B to D then requires a drift correction itself, which is determined in the same way as the previous figure (Figure 34). The course to steer (Co.(T)) between the thermals of 053° T represents a very large drift correction; staying on track could well be impossible for an inexperienced pilot.

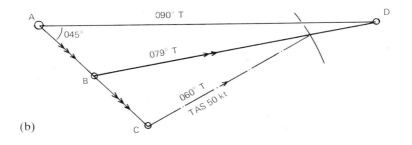

(b)

The following table gives the effect of wind of different values on an equilateral triangle for a range of task speeds:

Note: the triangular flight for which the calculations below are made is the same as the one in Fig. 36; the assumed cross-country speed is 60 kph.

wind strength (kt)	time taken (minutes)			
	1st leg	2nd leg	3rd leg	Total
0	100	100	100	300
5	109	111	87	307
10	120	125	77	322
15	143	150	68	361
20	173	192	62	427

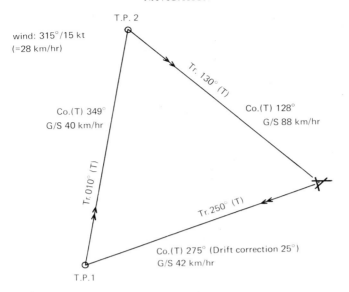

Figure 36. Allowances for wind; flight time estimates. The 5 hours which it would take to complete the task if there were no wind would become:

First leg	2 : 23
Second leg	2 : 30
Third leg	1 : 08
	6 : 01

For these sums, the wind direction used is 315°; in terms of total time, however, the direction does not matter for an equilateral triangle. In practice the wind strength would be limiting when the thermal strength – strictly the achieved rate of climb – was not sufficient to make any progress into wind. The minimum rate of climb to make progress into wind is dealt with on page 146.

Armed with this knowledge of the compass and the effects of the wind, some practical situations where its use may be of value can be considered.

Setting Course

It will always be the case when setting off from a familiar site – usually the home airfield – that there is some familiar landmark on, or near to, track towards which a pilot will fly. This is understandable enough but what should be done as a cross check is to refer to the compass; this serves two purposes:

1.   To calibrate the instrument against a known track (useful if it is in error).
2.   To give a first approximation of drift correction.

The first check will be of use when over unfamiliar country, and the second will avoid a common error of failing to correct for drift which leads to drifting to the downwind side of the track. The longer the delay in making this drift correction, the larger it must be in the later stages of the leg; ultimately the turning point would be approached almost into wind, if no correction were made.

Gliding to a destination or turning point
If the glide to the turning point is started from an off-track position, then most experienced pilots will be able to tell at a glance of the map the track required and correct this for variation, compass error and drift. It may be easier however to adjust the previously determined figure by using the one-in-sixty rule.

Map preparation/folding
The scale of the map is significant in deciding how to prepare it. If a small scale map, say 1 : 1,000,000, is used, then it is almost certain that the map can be folded to make the whole of the task visible. Generally however the one-million map has too little detail except for places like South Africa or Australia where there isn't much detail on the ground anyway. With half- or quarter-million maps, folding is nearly always necessary and the folds should be arranged 'concertina-fashion'.

Finally, when the map, in the concertina folds, is open at any two adjacent folds it can be folded in half again; this gives a maximum map size of eleven inches by nine when folded and eighteen inches by eleven when changing from one side to the next (for the UK half-million map). It may take the experience of a 'cockpit full of map' to convince you about the value of this method.

Map folding

The aim is to fold the map to an easily handleable size yet at the same time make it easy to 'turn the pages'. The following method is probably not unique, but it works well in practice. The numbers refer to the plates.

1. One of the first things that can be done is to make the map smaller by cutting off the margins. This means, however, that you cannot make reference to the legend or scales, and you will not know the date of the Aeronautical Information unless you note it elsewhere.

2. Then fold the map in half with the map face inwards. Generally this first fold will be parallel to the bottom edge although in some cases (e.g. Scotland), if mainly one side of the map is used, then the first fold will be parallel to the side.

3. Having made the first fold it should be reversed, so that the map is face outwards. (Most folds will be reversed.)

4. Now fold the map in half again, parallel to the shorter edge this time, and again reverse the fold.

5. Open the map out to half size (as in 3).

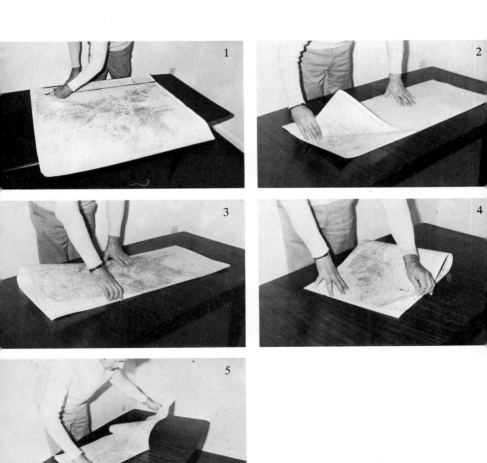

6. Fold each vertical edge to the centre; in Plate 6 the right-hand side is being folded, while the left-hand side has already been done.

7. The edges which meet together in the centre should be folded out as shown. The right-hand side is shown being folded, the left-hand side is already done.

8. Turn the map over, putting the sections already folded next to the table.

9. Fold the outside edges (now comprising six thicknesses of paper) to the centre again; the actual fold is only made through two thicknesses.

10. The map should now look as in Plate 10, having been folded into eight parts, concertina fashion.

11. At this stage it may be small enough for your needs and if either the left- or right-hand outside panel is being used then it can be reduced to this size.

12. It will be twice the size shown in Plate 11 if any of the panels in between are required – it may not fold back on itself too well if you try to half the size again.

13. To reduce the size still further fold the top edge to the bottom (or *vice versa* of course). This fold will be made downwards to keep the part of the map which interests you to the front.

    Before you can make a sideways fold in order to change to the next panel this last fold must be opened out.

    If for most of the time the middle portion of the map is being used, further folds can be made to make this part more readily accessible.

14. Open the map out completely, laying it face down; fold the top and bottom edges to the centre.

15. When complete, the pages can be turned as in a book (provided that all the folds have been reversed) and any part of the map is easily accessible.

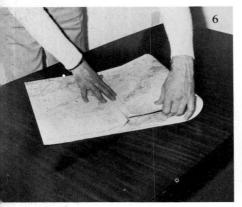

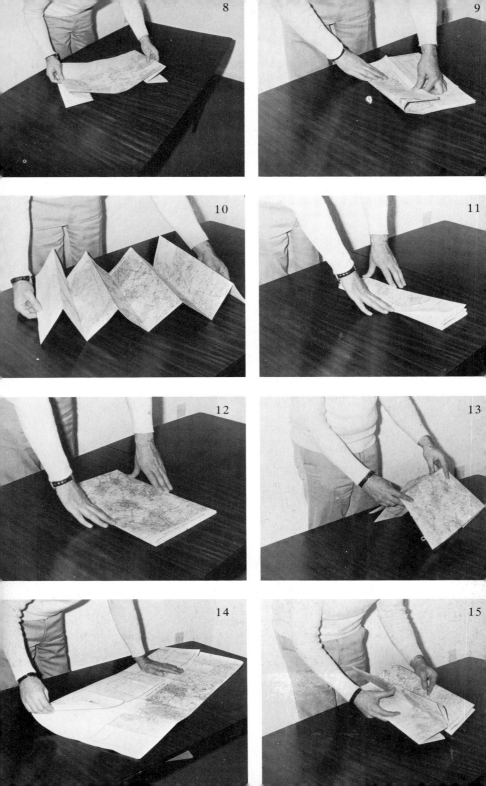

The standard (paper) finish should be marked with a soft pencil but if it is to be used frequently rubbing out the old line may take the surface off the paper and make the map less easy to read. Most pilots who use their maps a lot will prefer their map covered with a transparent plastic film. Maps can be bought with this finish already on them, but some pilots prefer to cover them themselves after putting distance circles around their home airfield at every 5 nautical miles or so (or 10 km) which simplifies final glide calculations. With a plastic-surface map a chinagraph pencil can be used direct, although again some pilots prefer to apply Sellotape along track lines before marking up. A note of caution when marking with a chinagraph pencil; avoid too thick a line; features can easily be obscured. A few pilots are reluctant to put a line on the map at all – their reason being that they tend to stay too near to track, to the detriment of staying with the best soaring conditions.

A pilot who is under-confident about his navigating ability may well have this tendency, and if this is so it may be better to put two lines – say six or eight nautical miles apart – equally spaced about the track (Figure 37).

The course-to-steer figures used in Figure 37 are those calculated in Figure 36 and are in degrees (true), that is, they are not corrected for variation or compass error. The photographic zone is an arc of ninety degrees equally disposed either side of the line bisecting the angle between the inbound and outbound legs and is only shown for the first turning point.

The last information to put on the map is for the final glide. Very few pilots in the early stage of their cross-country experience ever learn how far the glider will go, unless, by chance, having it in mind to minimise the retrieve, they glide towards home after the last lift.

In this situation, the work-load may be quite high, especially as one gets down to field selection height, and this is not conducive to getting 'fixes' and using the final-glide calculator. The minimum information required is speed for maximum distance (best L/D speed for the estimated wind). Figure 38 shows the markings.

With the map properly folded and marked up the actual navigation can now be considered.

One of the most useful preparation exercises is a winter-time one of poring over maps and dreaming of next season's flights, be they 100 kilometres or 500. Using both the quarter- and half-million maps, consider the features that you will use, in a band six to eight

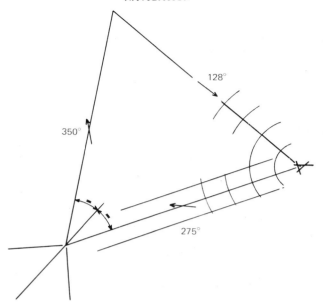

Figure 37. Marking the map. The additional information that might be included is:

(a) Directional information, the computed course to steer if this has been determined, and if not, the appropriate wind. The forecast wind will usually be given at 2,000 feet and 5,000 feet, and as this is a typical height band for a cross-country flight, then the average of the two will be a reasonable compromise.

(b) The sector from which each turning point will be photographed. It may well be helpful to have a separate map – probably a quarter-million – for this purpose, but if not the sector should be marked as shown (for more details on turning point photography see Appendix 3).

miles wide along each track. It is likely that the number of features chosen on the quarter-million map will be too many, and on the half-million seemingly too few. Indeed it may be better to plan the flight initially on the smaller scale map to avoid the risk of 'over-navigating', that is, trying to be exactly certain of one's position all the time. First look at the features chosen on the half-million, and then on the quarter-million, and see how much more detail is evident.

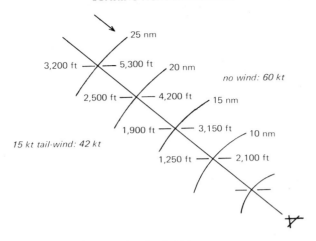

Figure 38. Marking the map for final glides.
The height values on the left are for best glide angle with a 15-kt tail-wind and a glide speed of 42 kt; the values on the right are for a glide speed of 60 kt (speed appropriate to a 2-kt rate of climb). The belief of most pilots in the glider's performance and the final glide calculations would be stretched to the limit in setting off on such a final glide, yet failure to do such calculations beforehand has resulted in many a pilot failing to complete a task, Silver 'C' or Gold 'C' distance, when it was actually possible.

A sample cross-country
The task chosen to examine in detail is a 180-kilometre triangle, Lasham/Devizes Castle/Didcot Railway Station/Lasham. The flight is described, along with photographs taken on an actual flight, in the following pages.

The ability to navigate well is only gained as a result of experience – the demands on the concentration of a pilot with no practical experience will be considerable, while the experienced pilot knows just where he is the whole of the time. For the pilot learning to navigate, there is much to be gained from poring over maps and discussing various features with more experienced pilots.

As well as this a consciousness of time and direction, particularly changes, even small ones, of direction, will all help in keeping a check of one's position. This orientation is most important when good features are few and far between, when attempts to navigate by map-reading over open country will have limited success, and may often be to the detriment of soaring considerations.

A Sample Cross-Country

This series of photographs is best viewed in conjunction with the standard aeronautical charts – both the half-million (sheet 2171CD) and the quarter-million (Sheet 16, Southern England) on which the track lines should be drawn. Starting and finishing at Lasham, the turning points are:
  a) Devizes Castle, which is just in the western edge of the town and just south of the canal.
  b) Didcot Railway Station, which is just to the east of the railway junction and to the north-east of the town.

Leg 1: Lasham to Devizes Castle: 38 nm, 70 km

Looking west there is little to be seen in the way of obvious landmarks, or, indeed, any at all! However the track line is some fifteen degrees to the north of west and from the map the first obvious feature is the motorway (M3). 1

	Feature	Dist. along Track (nm)*	Remarks	Plate	Suitability of Feature
1	Motorway	5	Line feature – check the angle at which you cross it; distinctive junctions make possible a track fix.	2	Good

*'L' and 'R' indicate a feature is Left or Right of track.

2   This view is to the right of track and at right-angles to it. In practice this is still in the local area (i.e. you should know where you are) but it still serves as a useful 'fix' with the roundabout over the motorway, the converging main road and the edge of the town (Basingstoke).

3   With the last fix (Plate 2) behind you it is natural to look for the next feature. This view of a large wood is looking along track but the glider is now two miles or so south of track. The wood isn't too obvious on the half-million map but the roads to the south-east and north of it are. Interestingly the railway line which you have chosen as the next feature isn't visible at all.

2	Railway line	8	Supplementary to (1) but unnecessary as (3) is probably visible.	4	

Looking south. The reason that the line is invisible is obvious in this picture; the railway line passes under the road and is running in a cutting. This is not evident from the map however. The message should be obvious – 'don't expect to see a line feature until quite close to it'. Note that the glider's position is still south of track by a couple of miles. From the map the next obvious feature is a town.

3	Whit-church	12L	Distinguished by railways (one E-W, one N-S, disused), and dual carriageway to the South.	5 6	Good

It is just conceivable that the town at 9R (Overton, not named on the half-million map) might be misidentified, but checking of the road/railway configuration in relationship to the town would soon convince you of your error.

The track line takes us just north of the town which should be quite distinctive. This view, looking south, shows the town and additional features which confirm it. (Remember that this practice of confirming a feature by others is a good one even if you are convinced that the town is the right one.) The sweep of the by-pass to the south and west of the town (view looking south) and the railway which lies east-west are sufficient confirmation, but notice also the disused railway.

6   The same town from the other side (south-east of it, looking north-west);
     the features are much less obvious – the by-pass being the only prominent
     one.
         The next prominent feature is a large town well south of track.

4	Andover	17L	A large town and 3 nm S of track; it is the biggest *en route*; with an airfield to the W, it can hardly be mistaken for any other town. The airfield is an all-grass field (local knowledge).*	7	

7   The glider is south of track again and this is a view looking south. This
     airfield is just to the west of Andover and is fairly obvious. Note that it is
     marked as a helicopter airfield on the half-million map. The town is con-
     cealed beneath the glider's wing.
         From this position the glider needs to be headed north-west to regain
     track and, ideally, to get slightly north of it in order to 'skirt' the Danger
     Area D125.

*Airfield layouts, runways and nature of the surfaces, may be found in the *Air
Touring Flight Guide* (see Bibliography).

5	Thruxton Airfield	21L	Three tarmac runways (not usable); this is a difficult airfield to pick out esp. in cloud shadow; also, one would be looking into sun which never makes it easy.	—	
6	Wood; N of Ludgershall	22	This wood actually serves as a better reference than the town to the S. This wood is on its own, on track and distinctive in shape.	8	Good

The wood – two or three miles across – is distinctive in shape, as a comparison of map and picture shows. The direction of view here is to the north-west and there are no obvious features beyond the wood for the time being at least (although the map shows several). 8

There is now need to divert slightly north of track to avoid entering the Danger Area D125 (marked by the line with the hatching); the position of the town (Ludgershall) is part concealed by this hatching and the best landmark will be Pewsey.

7	Pewsey	29R	A distinctive town lying between two areas of high ground. The canal and railway confirm that it is Pewsey; the white horse marked on the half-million map is not identifiable.	9	Good

9   With the wooded area behind, the next feature to be used is a town – Pewsey. This is a view of the town looking east (almost) with railway line running from top to bottom of the picture. The white horse which is obvious on the map cannot be seen at all. The canal to the north of the town (highlighted) is just visible in the top right-hand corner of the picture.

10 White horses and similar features are visible from a few miles away – especially if the sun is shining on them. A note of caution however; look at the general lie of the land in case this sort of feature is on a slope which is away from you and possibly hidden from view altogether. From here Devizes is only a few miles away and a 'lead-in' feature (line) would be useful if the town cannot be seen.

From Pewsey, Devizes should be visible; if not there are two line features, railway and canal leading in the general direction. The castle at Devizes – a turning point – is not shown on the half-million map and the quarter-million locates it at the western edge of the town.

8	Devizes (Castle)	38	Identified by canal, track of former railway and the Castle.	12	Good

The railway line goes well to the south, but the track of a disused railway   11
goes through the town and the junction between the two is clearly visible.

It may take a little time to find the Castle (the turning point) unless you have   12
been briefed as to its position; it is on a small wooded hill in the foreground
of the picture (ringed). This view is taken from much further away than
would be necessary or desirable for a turning point photograph but it is
almost in the middle of the photographic zone.

With the turning point photographed the new track is to the north-east
(roughly) over high ground, with no prominent features before Marlborough.

Leg 2: Devizes Castle to Didcot Railway Station 32 nm, 59 km

13   With no features to aim for it is important to use the compass and maintain a heading (080; this photo is looking ahead). It is easy to be misled or tempted into using features which may not be reliable. However there is one feature that does stand out (see Plate 14).

1	Bow in Canal	3	Clearly visible and a useful feature for indicating track line.	—	Good
2	Hill	Spot height (964 ft) 5L	Difficult to distinguish from other hills.	—	Poor
3	White Horse to NW of	4L	Neither visible (if the glider is on track) because the ground slopes away.	—	No good at all
4	White Horse to SE of track	5R		—	
5	Distinctive Road Junction	6L	The quarter million-map shows a roundabout	14	Good

Looking north. This distinctive road junction half-way from the turning 14
point to Marlborough becomes a positive fix (especially when compared
with the quarter-million map); the cloud shadow makes it rather less
evident.

The confident navigator might well not look for this, regarding the next
town as soon enough to confirm his position.

| 6 | Marl-borough (and White Horse) | 11R | In a visibility of 15 nm town not visible until within 5 nm; White Horse very small and quite difficult to spot. Note: all the symbols on the map are the same size – not so the features on the ground. Marlborough can be confirmed by the distinctive wood lying between roads to the SE of the town. | 15 | Good |

15 Looking south-east. It would seem natural to confirm Marlborough by its
    white horse; although the map symbol is the same size as all the others the
    actual landmark is not. The large, roughly-triangular, wood beyond the
    town with roads to either side is distinctive however.
        From here the confident navigator would strike out and not be concerned
    with small details.

7	Lighted Mast (500 ft) to 1200 ft ASL	18R	A feature with a symbol that stands out well on the map but nothing like so well from the air. Even when location on the disused airfield has been found, the mast will still not be easy to see.	16	Poor
8	Membury Airfield/ Motorway Service Area	18R	A useful combined feature; the motorway visible from 4 to 5 nm. The line feature (M4) gives distance along track and the Service Area confirms whether on track or not.	16	Good

Motorways are prominent features and this one is made more so by the 16
disused airfield (Membury) on which is built a service area (not evident
from the map). What would appear to be obvious from the map is the tall
lighted obstruction – a mast – but this could only be seen with difficulty in
the prevailing light, and none of the photographs revealed it.

   Remember that in crossing a line feature the angle that you make to it is a
useful confirmation of heading – but don't forget the allowance being made
for drift!

The turning point – Didcot Railway Station – cannot be identified from this
distance but, given good visibility, the power station might be visible from
10 or 15 nm; a diversion N of track (via Wantage) was made to avoid the
restricted area (R14/2.5) which goes up to a height of 2,500 feet AMSL.
Given the conditions, it would have been better to stay on track and fly over
the top of this restricted area. On this occasion, the cooling towers at the
power station were only visible from a point slightly west of Wantage.

9	Wantage/ Grove Airfield	26L	Combined features of this sort, if not quite unique, provide very reliable fixes. Note: disused airfields might be quite difficult to identify on their own.	18	Good

17 A distinctive view of the cooling towers at Didcot.

18 Looking north. The glider was steered north of track here to avoid the restricted area (R14, which extends up to a height of 2400 feet AGL). Wantage is confirmed by the disused airfield to the north of it.

10	Railway Line (from N of Grove Air-field to Didcot)		An excellent lead-in feature to the turning point.	—	Good

| 11 | Didcot Railway Station | 33 (tp) | Although one might find the Station by looking for it at Didcot, a quarter-million map shows its position to the N of the town at the junction of 3 railway lines. The middle of the photographic zone is when the glider is flying parallel to the main railway line. | 19 | |

This general view (looking south) is not one that a 'press-on' competition   19
pilot would ever see but it does show clearly the railway configuration which
enables the station to be pin-pointed. The optimum view would be from
much closer (in the sense of distance past the turning point) as in the next
plate.

20   Looking south-west. Even this is taken from well beyond the turning point
     but it is in the middle of the photographic zone – looking at right-angles to
     the main-line railway.
         From now on the last leg is fairly straightforward from the navigational
     point of view.

Some of the principles of map reading should have become clear from the
foregoing notes on the various features used. The final leg will bring out one
or two more and show that even using the half-million map, there may be a
tendency to use more features than are necessary and consequently spend
too much time navigating. The last leg of the flight can be simplified to
steering a course and keeping the river (Thames) on the left and then the
areas of water west of Reading also two or three miles to the left. The
motorway, and soon after the road/railway/canal/river feature, which runs
from Newbury to Reading, gives a fix for distance along track and may, with
careful map reading, give a fix for left or right of track. Such detail is
probably unnecessary however; the slightly less accurate approach of Newbury on the right and Reading on the left should be adequate. The line
feature between them will identify the glider's position as past the airway
and there the pilot can climb to a height for final glide. Note that at this
position the glider should not be lower than 2,400 feet (AMSL) – more of
this later in the section on Controlled Airspace.

This principle of less detailed navigation is illustrated in the remaining
plates.

Looking south-east. With the river (Thames) on the left direction can easily   21
be maintained; distance along track is given by the town on the left (note
the railway as well) but the obvious distance-along-track feature to use in
this case is the motorway again.

The motorway stands out clearly from a distance but it is not necessary to   22
'search in the distance' for this sort of feature; if you maintain heading it is
bound to appear sooner or later. Note that a useful indication of the wind is
apparent in this picture.

23 A view to the left of track at this stage shows the expanses of water to the west of Reading. The navigator who 'aims to keep it simple' would settle here for 'between Reading and Newbury'.

24 Of academic interest is this view to the west which shows (from right to left) a road (dual carriageway becoming single), railway, canal and finally a river which fixes the glider as being almost exactly on track and also gives the distance to run for a final glide check.

This view (looking south-west) shows the motorway and a spur (in the foreground) just to the east to Basingstoke; this again pinpoints the glider as almost exactly on track which would be useful if the airfield could not be seen.

25

Home again! A well-judged final glide would give a much more oblique view of the airfield – who took a last thermal that wasn't necessary?

26

Controlled airspace

One of the problems facing any pilot nowadays on the majority of cross-country flights is keeping clear of, or complying with the regulations regarding, 'controlled airspace'. A look at any United Kingdom map, except perhaps for the remoter parts of the country, will show a profusion of areas in many shapes and sizes which have different rules and regulations applying to them.

It is a pilot's responsibility to comply with these rules and regulations; failure to do so can, and occasionally does, result in prosecution. Attitudes towards the rules vary, one of the simplest is 'don't go into any area which might have some control, be it restricted or prohibited, even if entitled to do so'. Such an attitude keeps an individual pilot in the clear, but if all glider pilots subscribed to it then 'custom and practice' might be used as a justification for changing the status of a particular piece of airspace which glider pilots at present have the right to fly through, to exclude them from it.

A better attitude, to my mind, is to take a positive approach and *use* the airspace which one is entitled to enter. In between the extremes ('stay out at all costs', and 'stand up for one's rights'), there is, perhaps, a compromise where good airmanship plays a part. There is no better example of the need for this than in the Military Air Traffic Zone which is shown in Figure 39.

Any airfield with an Air Traffic Control (ATC) unit or providing an Aerodrome Flight Information Service (AFIS) has the protection that an ATZ provides; within this airspace a number of rules* apply:

1.   Make all turns to the left (unless ground signals show otherwise).
2.   When landing, leave other aircraft clear on their left.

Glider pilots should be sure to establish whether they have the right to land at any airfield they might consider using.

While the glider pilot is entitled to fly in the MATZ (but not the ATZ), he should, as a point of airmanship, appreciate the likely

---

* See *Rules of the Air and Air Traffic Control Regulations* (SI 1985/1714) for full details.

activity within this zone. In Figure 39 the dotted lines represent the path of an aircraft making an instrument let down and approach. Even if the weather is 'gin-clear' it should be assumed that the military pilot is far too busy to keep a look-out, and common sense dictates that this is not a good place to linger.

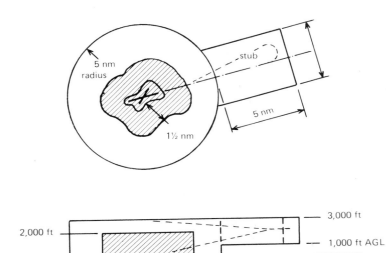

Figure 39. Military Air Traffic Zone.
Within the MATZ is another zone called an Air Traffic Zone (ATZ) which extends up to 2,000 ft AGL and 1½ nm from the airfield boundaries. The glider pilot's rights extend to flying in the MATZ but not, generally, in the ATZ, unless there is a gliding club operating there.

Visual Meteorological Conditions (VMC) and Visual Flight Rules (VFR)
Visual meteorological conditions are weather conditions in which an aircraft can comply with visual flight rules; there are three elements to this rule:

Above 3,000 feet:
One nautical mile horizontally from cloud, and
one thousand feet vertically from cloud, and in a flight visibility of five nautical miles.

Below 3,000 feet (outside controlled airspace and Special Rules Airspace*)
Clear of cloud and inside of the surface and, in a flight visibility of three nautical miles.

Note: The meaning of 'flight visibility' is the visibility forward from the flight deck of an aircraft in flight with the obvious implication of being able to see in the direction one is going rather than out to one side.

These rules are different if flying faster than 140 kt, but this is unlikely in a glider.

A clear understanding of this Rule† and its various applications is very important to glider pilots, because if it can be complied with, then the glider can penetrate certain types of controlled airspace – in the United Kingdom, notably airways and Special Rules Airspace.

The next important point for a pilot to understand is the alternative ways of defining the vertical limits of controlled airspace and some of the terms used in this context.

Ground level is clear enough, and upper limits of airspace in the UK will *never* be specified as height above ground level (AGL). The word 'height' is always used in relation to ground level. If an altimeter is set to read height, it will always be in relation to a particular airfield.

Sea level (more strictly 'mean sea level') is used as the datum for the base of lower level airspace. The abbreviation AMSL – above mean sea level – is the normal presentation; heights given above mean sea level are *altitudes* (ALT on maps).

Flight Levels and Transition Levels. Above a certain altitude – known as the Transition Level – all height references are relative to a particular pressure datum. Atmospheric pressure measured at airfields and corrected to a corresponding pressure at sea level varies over the earth's surface, and even over relatively short dis-

---

* Special Rules Zones (SRZs) and Special Rules Areas (SRAs).
† Statutory Instruments (SI 1985 No. 1714); see also p. 174
  These Rules are available to glider pilots in the BGA publication *Laws and Rules for Glider Pilots*.

tances it can change by a significant amount. The consequence of this is that two aircraft passing each other from different points of departure might have different altitudes indicated but actually be at the same level. This is unacceptable from the point of view of flight safety.

To avoid this state of affairs, above a certain level (the Transition Level), all aircraft adjust their altimeters to the same sub-scale setting – 1013 millibars – so that their 'altitudes', now known as 'Flight Levels' can be used to ensure vertical separation. Flight Levels can be defined as altimeter readings in hundreds of feet measured from a pressure datum of 1013.2 mb. Flight Level zero is located at the atmospheric pressure level of 1013.2; Flight Level (FL) 55 corresponds to 5500 ft indicated with the standard sub-scale setting. This will be made clearer by an illustration. Figure 40:

For practical purposes a glider pilot flying around his home airfield will have the altimeter set to zero before take off. In aeroplane flying, this pressure setting is known as QFE. This figure, if set on the sub-scale setting, would mean that the altimeter gave height above the airfield.

Flying cross-country, most glider pilots will set their altimeter to give height above sea level ('altitude') and this is known as QNH.

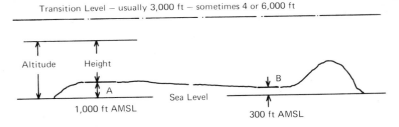

Figure 40a. Altimeter settings for height and altitude.
Suppose the *sea level pressures* at A and B are 1020 mb and 1010 mb; the corresponding pressures at airfield height can be determined (approximately) using the conversion rule of 27 ft = 1 mb
    1000 ft. is equivalent to 37 mb
     300 ft. is equivalent to 11 mb
Bearing in mind that the pressure reduces with increasing height, then the airfield pressures are:
    at A   1020 − 37 = 983
    at B   1010 − 11 = 999 mb
The airfield and sea level pressures are shown in Figure 40b.

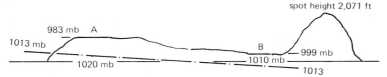

Figure 40b.
Here the pressure level – 1013 – is shown; it is above sea level at airfield A
and below sea level at B. It is this pressure data from which flight levels are
measured.

An aeroplane pilot flying cross-country will adjust this setting as he
changes regions – known as Altimeter Setting Regions – updating
the setting from broadcast or transmitted information. The advantage of QNH for cross-country flying is that terrain clearance can be
readily determined by subtracting from one's altitude the terrain
height – given as a spot height on the maps. Referring to the
previous figure (Figure 40), an aircraft from A at 3,000 ft (altitude)
would have an indicated terrain clearance at X of 3,000 − 2,071 =
929 ft. In reality, however, that clearance is reduced because the sea
level pressure at B near to the hill is 1010 and the altimeter is set to
1020. An altimeter set at 1020, in a pressure of 1010, will read zero
below sea level, by a distance corresponding to 10 mb. So at B, the
actual altitude of the aircraft is 270 ft less (10 mb = 270 ft) and the
terrain clearance is only 929 − 270 = 659 ft. This point, it should be
noted, is an academic one in gliding; it should, however, serve to
increase your understanding of the altimeter.

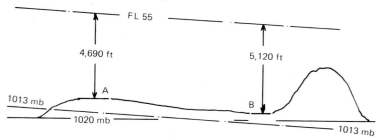

Figure 41. Altimeter setting for Flight Levels.
At (A):
1013 is 7 mb (190 ft) above sea level, therefore:
FL 55 is equivalent to 5690 ft AMSL or 4690 ft AGL.
At (B):
1013 is 3 mb (80 ft) below sea level, therefore:
FL 55 is equivalent to 5420 ft AMSL or 5120 ft AGL.

Flight Levels

If you want to relate your vertical position relative to the base of an airway, which is given as a Flight Level, then the easiest way to do this is to adjust the sub-scale to indicate 1013. Alternatively, the height or altitude of the airway base can be calculated using the conversion factor, 1 mb = 27 ft.

Extremes of pressure (at sea level) can range from about 970 to 1040 mb, which gives an actual variation in the base of an airway by as much as 1900 ft (these extremes of pressure would not usually give soaring conditions).

A practical look at the various sorts of controlled airspace affecting a typical cross-country flight will show the nature of the problems it creates. The cross-section of the flight in Figure 42 makes the assumption that the glider stays on track; with some diversions, the conflicts would be less.

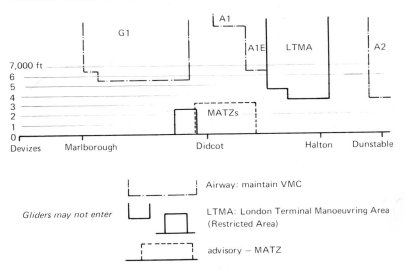

Figure 42. Cross-section of a cross-country and the controlled air-space.

5 Field Selection and Field Landing

Nowadays, the field landing is not regarded as part of a cross-country flight, at least, not of a successful one. Talk to the pundits, and you may well find that they haven't landed out for a year or two. The reason, of course, is that they abandon the task if the weather does not look too good en route.

Sadly, this state of affairs has the effect of offering an aspiring cross-country pilot a readily accepted excuse or justification (to himself and others) for not continuing with a task. A lack of determination and/or confidence is often the real reason behind the failure to press on. Another factor that may undermine a pilot's confidence is early cross-countries in which an out-landing was not necessary. Silver 'C' distance flights in particular are often declared to airfield goals, and although a goal flight is a much more satisfying experiences, it does preclude the confidence-building experience of a field landing.

Perhaps one of the most valuable second cross-country flights a pilot can have is a failed triangle, which gives him both the experience of rounding a turning point or two, and the confidence of a successful field landing. That confidence will not, of course, last for ever, and even quite experienced pilots will admit to being pleased at having landed out – because it restores their confidence. An ordered approach to field selection and landing is an essential part of any pilot's ability and the following summary* will help in this respect:

---

* The summary is available as a pocket-sized card from the British Gliding Association.

Field Landing Briefing

1. *2,000 ft.* If landing appears probable, fly to a suitable area, preferably flat and unobstructed; remember you'll cover far more ground if you fly downwind.

2. *By 1,500 ft.* Pick an area with two or three potentially suitable fields: consider the surrounding terrain.

(a) Are there hills to create turbulence or surface wind problems?
(b) Are there high tension cables, masts or other large obstacles?
(c) Does the ground slope visibly? If it does, it's too steep!
(d) Stay orientated with wind direction experienced during the cross-country, relate to sun position.

3. *1,200 to 1,000 ft.* Select your field, considering the following:

   (a) *Surface wind.* Assess the wind by means of your drift or by smoke. Always aim to land in a direction which will give you a substantial headwind component.

   (b) *Field length.* Remember the apparent size of any field is seen relative to the size of those surrounding it. Know the topography of the country over which you are flying. A *good* field for a modern glider would be 5–600 yards long with relatively unobstructed boundaries.

   (c) *Obstructions.* Obstructions cut from the usable field length at least ten times the height at which you clear them. Trees and buildings will create turbulence.

   (d) *Slope.* Any visible down-slope in the field is unacceptable. A similar up-slope would be acceptable, though a serviceable wheel brake is then desirable. Examine surrounding fields for slope indications.

   (e) *Surface.* Look for fields in the following order:
      (i) Stubble.
      (ii) Grass, but beware of strip grazing indicating electric fences; any shading in grass surface almost certainly indicates the presence of fencing.
      (iii) Short crop. The surface should appear more brown than green.
      (iv) Other cropped fields may present a hazard on landing. Remember, half-ripe crops may look like stubble. Consider the season!

(f)   *Stock.* Sheep panic, run, and sometimes jump up. Cows are curious, horses bolt. A solitary cow is probably a bull! Try to avoid fields with stock in them.

These are summarised in the mnemonic: Size, Slope, Surface, Stock.

4.   *By 800 ft AGL.* Position the glider well upwind and well to one side of your field – visualise the length of the downwind leg at your home airfield. Use pre-selected ground reference points to maintain orientation when positioning. Be conscious of the tendency to cramp your circuit, and plan to avoid doing so.

5.   *Base Leg Position.* Plan to be abeam of your touchdown by 4–500 ft. Resist the common tendency to position the base leg too close – plan for half-brake approach. Select a safe approach speed. Excessive speed in a modern glider will usually result in overshooting the field. Allow an adequate margin of height over obstructions. Once you are certain you can safely clear them, use full airbrake to achieve early touchdown. Aim for minimum touchdown speed on rough surfaces. Ground looping is common when landing in crop. Concentrate on keeping the wings level, and retract flaps if necessary.

This summary will serve as a basis for a deeper examination of some of the factors involved.

Heights

The heights recommended are appropriate for the majority of pilots in their early field landings. They will almost certainly be reduced as a pilot gains experience, as the stories of competition 'low scrapes' and other 'bar stories' bear witness. What the average pilot does not appreciate is that the competition pilot has probably the ability to pick field as he attempts to 'scrape' away; the task demands very little of his concentration and the work-load in this respect is low. He may also be competent to get into a much smaller field than the average pilot and, perhaps the most critical factor, he is prepared to take chances in his bid to win.

For the majority of pilots, the heights recommended should be adhered to, but here is a note of caution to the under-confident: do not add 'five hundred feet for the wife and kids'. If you do, the chances of a successful field landing are probably reduced. At two thousand five hundred feet, you should still be concentrating on soaring, flying towards sunlit ground with likely clouds overhead. You might have an eye on a likely area, or, more positively, be aware of the *areas over which you will not fly*. The thousand feet or so that you have to spare will take you four or five miles in a one-in-twenty-five glider.

In a hilly or undulating terrain, flying downwind to a 'suitable area' presents a problem. The fields of which you have the best view slope towards you; that is they are downhill when into wind.

The last word about heights is that unless you know exactly where you are and therefore the height of the terrain, then the altimeter cannot be relied on. It is usual to set the altimeter to read height above sea level (AMSL). This gives the simplest of sums (altitude minus terrain height equals height above the ground), and sums must be simple if you are to get them right in the air. However, unless you are completely lost, you should know the height above ground within a hundred feet or two; it is still best not to rely on the altimeter.

The area of potentially suitable fields may be less than ideal if there are hills which may create turbulence or variations in the surface wind – later this will be significant in terms of approach control and speed. In some areas more than others, there is a proliferation of cables, on large pylons, small pylons and poles; the latter are difficult to see and you should look for the poles rather than the wires. This type of potential obstruction may be an imaginary hazard rather than a real one, but if there is a need to modify the circuit to avoid them then they are too close to the field for comfort.

Assessment of slope should be made not just by looking at the field you have chosen, but also at the surrounding countryside as well. A pilot may be reluctant to do this for fear of losing sight of his field. Remember that if the slope is clearly visible from the air then it is probably too steep to land on. It is worth noting that slope may only be seen when viewed from a particular direction and so it is useful to fly around the chosen field/area and see it from different directions.

Throughout this stage it is essential to be, and remain, orientated with the chosen field and the wind direction. Relating the wind direction to the sun's position may help.

Selecting the field

By 1,200 ft, or 1,000 ft at the latest, the most suitable field should be chosen, having taken into account all the various factors. At this stage there are a number of pitfalls of which you should be aware.

Indecisiveness is the real risk and, strangely, this may be simply because there are too many 'possible' fields. If none of the fields stand out as ideal, a pilot may continue weighing up the pros and cons of each until it is too late to make an organised approach, let alone a circuit, into one of them.

Another awkward situation is making the choice of field too soon – say at 1,500 feet. Only when the glider is down to seven or eight hundred feet do the details that make it unsuitable show up – strip grazing with fences between strips or tall unripe crops that look like grass. The consequence of premature choice is a last-minute change of mind – usually when it is too late to organise an approach into an alternative field. There is a maxim that may serve to protect you from such a situation and that is:

A good approach into a poor field is better than a bad approach into a good one.

To this might be added:

Any decision is better than no decision at all.

The surface wind

When you have to land out, Murphy's Law applies. There is no indication of wind direction. For want of any obvious indications (smoke or occasionally the wind swaying tall crops), then the decision must be based on:

1. *The forecast wind.* The surface wind has a diurnal variation – that is it changes during the day – veering (clockwise change of direction) during the morning and backing (anti-clockwise) towards evening. The passage of a front of any sort will cause a change in direction.

2. *The drift experienced during the flight.* Of particular value is the drift noticed in the last desperate attempts to remain airborne. Although the work-load will be high in this instance, a quick check of one's position relative to, say, a farmhouse, will give the necessary information after a few turns.

3. The *final confirmation comes from an accurately flown circuit pattern* with the downwind leg parallel to the landing direction and

the base leg at right angles to it, during which drift correction, if necessary, will give a reasonable indication of wind direction.

Field length

The field chosen should be the longest available or, more specifically, the one with the longest into-wind run. To talk in terms of actual length may not be very meaningful; there are some parts of the country where two hundred and fifty yards is regarded as long. However, the smaller the field, the less the margin for error, and you always want the largest margin possible.

Assessment of length by relating a field to the spacing of telegraph (*not* electricity) poles (sixty-six yards) may be of value if time is available and the pilot is relaxed enough to do this. It is better, however, to know the areas where fields are small, and this you can find out by talking to experienced cross-country pilots. Instructors should know where *not* to send pilots on first or early cross-country flights.

Various features of the glider may also be significant in the selection of the field; if the approach angle is shallow – that is, the airbrakes are not very powerful – then even a tall hedge can effectively 'cut off' a hundred yards or so. If the glider has the wings set low on the fuselage, the ground-cushion effect is more significant than for a glider with a high wing (i.e. the glider will float a long way). This must be taken into account. Add poor speed control on the approach to these factors, then a field which might have been adequate may prove to be anything but!

On the benefit side is the fact that most modern gliders have very effective wheel brakes. If you have such a glider then it is worth bearing in mind the possibility of flying the glider on to the ground (as opposed to making a fully-held-off landing) and using the brake.

The undershoot/overshoot view

A view often expressed regarding a field landing is 'choose a field with a good undershoot and a good overshoot to it'. If this view is put forward on the premise that the pilot cannot guarantee landing in the field of his choice, then he should not even be flying across country (with the inherent risk of landing out).

When the field proves inadequate!

One of the facts of gliding life, as, perhaps, life in general, is that you 'only learn by your mistakes'. Let us suppose for the moment that 'it could happen to you'. If by some stroke of misfortune the field proves to be too small, then it may help if you have considered these alternatives:

1.   Landing with the undercarriage retracted.
2.   Deliberately landing heavily to dissipate as much of the glider's energy as possible.
3.   Ground looping. Many modern gliders with tail wheels and the centre of gravity well behind the main wheel are quite difficult to ground loop but once started it will be impossible to stop. The risk is probably greatest when harsh braking raises the tail wheel from the ground and directional control is lost.

Although the aircraft will almost certainly be damaged, the risks to the pilot are less than if the glider runs into the fence.

Obstructions
Most fields will have obstructions of some sort. If these are only a few feet high, they are of no consequence because the touch-down point aimed for will be some way into the field. Once the boundary fence is cleared, it will be usual to open the airbrakes fully and land short of the intended point – with the exception that if the field is very long the brakes might be closed to allow the glider to float along its length.

The same principle applies if there are higher obstructions, except that the higher they are the more the clearance that should be allowed. This is for the fairly obvious reason that obstructions create turbulence which may have an adverse effect on the approach. As a measure of the amount of field cut off by obstructions, ten times the height by which they are cleared is a reliable guide – fifty feet cuts off five hundred feet, or one hundred and sixty-seven yards – which may be half the length of an otherwise adequate field.

Slope
Slope, if detectable from the air, it must be emphasised, is acceptable only for an uphill landing, even to the extent of landing downwind. The judgement problems on both counts – slope and tail wind – should be recognised:

1. The round-out will have to be started slightly higher than usual because the glider has to be rotated through a larger angle than when landing on the level.
2. The perspective of the field will give the impression that the glider is high on the approach. To help appreciate this, think of a good approach to a level field and then visualise the significance on approach judgement of rotating the field towards you. It will appear that the glider is high on the approach and correction with the brakes may cause an under-shoot.
3. There may be turbulence, curl-over (turbulence in the lee of hills), or a marked gradient to make approach control more difficult.
4. Remember that if you are *gliding downwind, the fields you* will have the better view of slope towards you, and will be downhill for an into-wind approach.
5. The glider may well roll back and a serviceable wheel brake may be essential.

Surface

The most suitable field surface varies with the season. In the spring, the short crops in harrowed fields will offer the widest choice. After harvest time, stubble fields are by far the best, but there is a time just before cereal crops are ripe when they can look very like stubble which has been undersown with grass. Even at seven or eight hundred feet it can be difficult to tell the two apart, and the real protection comes from an awareness of crop state throughout the season: you do not have to be flying to notice this.

Grass fields are notoriously misleading if they are divided for strip-grazing; detection of the fences relies on the field having been used recently. If it has not, it will be difficult or impossible to tell. A pasture that has not been used as anything else for many years may well be rough and have tussocks. One particular variety of field is known as 'ridge and furrow'; there are certain parts of the country where this is, or was, the practice. The method of ploughing creates the undulations which may be as much as eighteen inches from peak to trough. To land across the ridges would almost certainly break the glider and landings must be made as in a ploughed field – along the furrows.

Fields with animals in them present problems which depend on the type of animal. The curiosity of cows is notorious, and you may well have to defend the glider against them until help arrives.

The circuit for field landing

All the problems related to planning the circuit for field landing are, once recognised, relatively easy to overcome. They stem, in the main, from habits formed at one's home airfield; some of them have been dealt with in Chapter 1, but additional problems are:

1. There are no familiar ground features in a field landing.
2. A reluctance to 'stand-off' from the chosen field and fly a circuit of the normal size; the 'mental block' is in trying to treat the actual field as an airfield – starting the circuit at the upwind end. As a defence against this, tell yourself how many fields you need to fly over on downwind leg, base leg and final approach to have it resemble the normal circuit. There is also the difficulty of resolving the two aims of flying around the field to see it from different angles and then getting far enough upwind without losing sight of it.
3. The tendency to make full-brake approaches because there has always been considerable overshoot area at one's home airfield – not so in the field landing case.
4. Caution, or lack of confidence, making one reluctant to fly a circuit of adequate size.
5. Tendency to fly a downwind leg parallel to the long edge of the field notwithstanding the fact that the into-wind direction may be the diagonal.
6. 'Making the approach look right' when the glider is much too close, by progressively lowering the nose, with failure to monitor airspeed, which increases. (If the airbrakes are very powerful, they can limit the increase.)
7. Poor speed control. This may be due to 6 or to insufficient monitoring. If conditions allow, reduce speed gradually in the final stages of the approach.

The final requirement is a well-controlled approach, which is essential for many field landings. It should be remembered that the manner of landing dealt with previously (see pages 29–30) is still a consideration.

Having landed in the field, the action to be taken depends on the circumstances – it might be too windy to get out of the glider for instance: better to wait for help than have it blow over – but all the after-landing considerations are dealt with in the section on retrieving and crewing. As a final word on field landings, the following code of conduct deals with one aspect of field landing which might be forgotten.

Code of Conduct for Glider Pilots when landing in fields *

If glider pilots are to continue to enjoy their sport, it is vital that the goodwill of farmers and land owners is retained. A great deal is owed to many farmers who have given help and consideration to pilots who have arrived in a field as uninvited guests.

Most cross-country flights in gliders are planned to end at an airfield; however it must be emphasised that if a pilot fails to reach his destination and has to make a forced landing in a field, he incurs certain responsibilities.

The following code is intended to be a reminder of the conduct expected of all pilots. It is essential that all pilots should be aware of this code before they are first cleared for cross-country flying and that they are reminded of it from time to time.

The Code

1. Select a field that is not only safe to land in but one which should cause the least possible inconvenience to the farmer.
2. Particular care should be taken when standing grass and cereal crops cover large areas of the countryside, for a landing in these will damage the crops as well as the glider.
3. Care should be taken to land as far away from livestock as possible.
4. Immediately after landing and securing the glider endeavour to discourage on-lookers from coming into the field. For this reason it is preferable not to land in a field adjoining a housing estate.
5. Contact the farmer, or his representative, and explain the circumstances of the forced landing. Pay for any telephone calls. If unable to find him at the time, obtain his name,

---

* Originally drawn up by the British Gliding Association in consultation with the National Farmers Union and first published in *Sailplane and Gliding* magazine.

address and telephone number and contact him without fail as soon as possible.

6. Keep the retrieve vehicle off the field if it is likely to do any damage, unless permission is obtained; it may be better to manhandle the glider to the vehicle.

7. Ensure that no animals escape while the gate is open and that all gates opened are properly closed before leaving.

8. If any damage has been done, exchange names and addressess with the farmer as well as giving the address of the insurers covering the glider. All gliders should be adequately insured against third-party risks.

The Glider's Performance

To get the most from your glider it is essential to understand something about its performance. Generally, this requires an understanding of the appropriate theory, but there are many pilots – some of them National Champions in their time – who profess to understand nothing of the theory. For a pilot who genuinely cannot understand the theory there is no point at all in persisting with explanations, even the simplest of which he cannot understand. Such a pilot may well become an intuitive flyer and go on to be a Champion, but generally some understanding of theory is desirable.

The starting point is to recognise the average pilot's shortcomings of technique in soaring conditions. A typical situation which almost every instructor would recognise is with the glider flying through 'sinking air' and the student being prompted to increase the speed, to get out of the sinking air as quickly as possible. That the student alone makes no significant increase in speed is hardly his fault if he does not understand the principles involved and has not received a specific prompt such as 'increase the speed to sixty knots'. As well as not understanding the theory, the student probably does not glance at the variometer often enough and so is unaware of the glider's rate of sink. To remedy this state of affairs requires a change of emphasis in training; if the student hopes to become a soaring pilot he should be encouraged to monitor the variometer reading. The only problem once this is encouraged is to stop him looking at it all the time (see 'Basic scan', page 19).

The calculation of the best speed to get out of sinking air is fairly involved and the understanding of it in depth requires mathematical proofs; a simplified approach is still convincing.

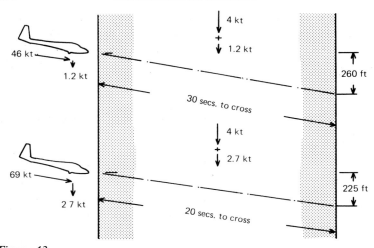

Figure 43
It is assumed that the glider flying at 46 kt and sinking at 1·2 kt flies into a patch of air sinking at 4 kt in which the glider's total sink rate would increase to 5·2 kt or 520 ft/min.* If it takes 30 seconds to cross then the height loss would be 260 ft.

If the speed were increased to 69 kt (a speed chosen arbitrarily to keep the times simple) then although the glider's sink rate increases to a total of 2·7 + 4 = 6·7 kt or 670 ft/min, the reduced time in the sinking air (20 seconds) means less overall height loss (225 ft).

In fact this arbitrary speed of 69 knots is very close to the theoretical speed for this situation for the particular glider. Excessive speed may result in greater height loss because the benefits from getting through the sinking air quickly are more than offset by the increase in the glider's sink rate. In practice, however, the speed can and should be increased in anticipation of the sinking air. This can be done on the premise that on leaving a thermal, sink will be encountered, and as in practice the speed between thermals will be higher than the circling speed, the normal technique on leaving a thermal will be appropriate to encountering sinking air.

To assist in flying the glider at the appropriate speed, information is presented to the pilot on a speed-to-fly ring which is fitted to the variometer. Its use can easily be taught, again without requiring any theoretical explanation. The previous example, Figure 43, can be re-examined to illustrate the point.

* 1 knot = 100 ft/min approximately.

The speed-to-fly ring is shown in Figure 44. A series of numbers –
usually in five knot steps – relate the airspeed to given rates of sink
so whatever value of sink rate the variometer pointer indicates,
there is an appropriate airspeed. In practice, it works like this (see
Figure 44 again).

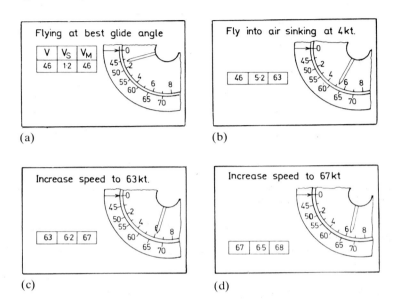

Figure 44. The speed-to-fly ring.
(a)   Before flying into the sinking air, the vario indicates 1·2 kt (the
       glider's rate of sink) and the airspeed should be 46 kt.
(b)   Once in the sinking air, the sink rate increases to 5·2 kt (4 + 1·2); the
       speed indicated on the ring is 63 kt. If, as it should, the glider's speed
       is increased to this value, a further increase in the total sink rate
       would be apparent (due to the fact that the faster the glider is flown
       the greater its sink rate will be).
(c)   With an increase in speed to 63 kt, the vario now shows 6·2 kt down
       and indicates that the speed should be 67 kt. If this further increase in
       speed were made then the sink rate would increase again to:
(d)   6·5 kt and an indicated speed of 68 kt.

The right speed is achieved by a series of approximations,
although in practice it would be done much more quickly by increasing speed to, say, five knots in excess of the first speed indicated (63
kt at (b)) which would make the whole sequence into a continuous

smooth adjustment of airspeed; on flying out of the sinking air the procedure would be reversed.

If this technique is to be used, it is essential to have a 'total-energy' variometer – one that is compensated for speed changes (see also pages 49–52). While a pilot may be taught to use a speed-to-fly ring at quite an early stage, it is likely – if he is at all curious – that he will want to know something about the way in which it is derived and other possibilities regarding its use and so a theoretical explanation becomes inevitable – see Appendix 1.

Glide ratio
Glide ratio is a simple measure of the glider's performance but as it is not presented directly to the pilot, it is best explained in other ways. Perhaps the simplest is to relate the glider's forward speed (air speed) to its vertical speed as indicated by the variometer. These two values at any one time can be used to determine the glide ratio.

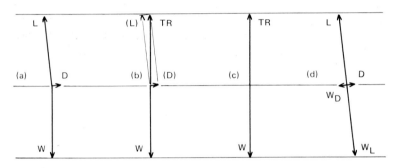

Figure 45. The forces on a glider in flight.
It should be noted that lift is defined as being at right angles to the direction of flight and drag parallel to it.
(a)   It is not immediately obvious that the forces acting on the glider are in balance.
(b)   To show the state of equilibrium or balance it is usual to combine the two forces L and D into one by a process known as resolution. The combined force is called the Total Reaction (TR) and is equal and opposite to the weight (W) as shown in (c).
(d)   An alternative way of presenting the forces on the glider is to 'resolve' the weight into two components or parts, one equal and opposite to lift and the other equal and opposite to drag.
The principle of balance used in the last diagram (d) is the same as in (c) except that the direction of the forces is now at right angles and parallel to the direction of flight.

A glider flying at 60 kt and sinking at 2 kt has a glide ratio of 1:30; this would only be a true value if the vario reading did not include any rising or sinking air and it was entirely accurate, which is not usually the case. The actual measurement of glide angle is not done so simply, requiring prolonged glides in undisturbed air and careful measurement of height loss at calibrated speeds.

The poor glider pilot may become confused by this explanation because he has heard glide angle expressed as a ratio of lift divided by drag, the L/D ratio. What is not appreciated is that the alternative ways of expressing it amount to the same thing so this is the first point to clear up.

The forces acting on a glider at constant speed are an equilibrium or balance; they are lift (L), drag (D) and weight (W). When represented diagrammatically it may not be at all obvious that these forces are in balance. See Figure 45.

The two forces, lift and drag, relate to glide angle; to understand this you need to dust off your geometry from school days. The next figure (46) shows the forces acting – weight is omitted as irrelevant to the explanation. Remember that lift is at right angles (perpendicular) to the direction of flight, and drag parallel to it.

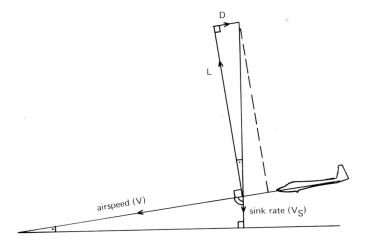

Figure 46. Glide angle related to the forces and to airspeed and sink rate. It should be evident by inspection of the diagram that the two angles indicated – the one between the glider's flight path and the horizontal and the other between the lift line and the vertical – are the same.

The geometric proof rests on the fact that the angles in a triangle together total 180°, as do the three angles to the left of the vertical line (one in the triangle, one of 90° and the other between the lift line and the vertical). Since both sets of three angles total 180° and in each set there is one right angle and one angle common to both, it follows that the remaining angles are the same.

An angle can be defined by the length of the sides of the triangle in which it is contained. The side opposite the angle in one case corresponds to drag and in the other height loss; the side adjacent to

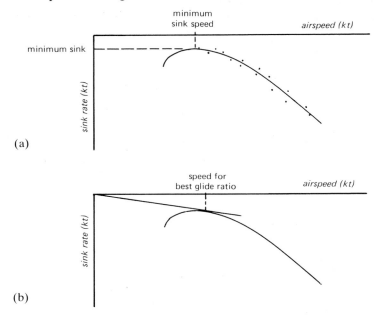

Figure 47. The 'polar': minimum sink and best glide.

(a)   Sink rate is shown, logically, downwards, and airspeed horizontally; a number of points will be determined at different airspeeds which will be joined together (and smoothed if necessary) to produce the graph called a 'polar'). The first point to identify in this diagram is the minimum sink rate.

(b)   A line has been drawn from the corner of this graph (known as the origin) to touch the curve of the polar which, by definition, makes it a tangent to that curve; if from the point of contact between the curve and the tangent a line is drawn upwards to cut the speed scale, then a triangle has been drawn and this represents the triangle from the previous diagram (Figure 46). If the scales of the two axes were the same, the angle would be true.

the angle in one case is lift and in the other drag so that the angle –
the glide angle – is given by either:

$$\frac{\text{Airspeed}}{\text{Sink rate}} \quad \frac{(V)}{(V_s)} \quad \text{or} \quad \frac{\text{Lift}}{\text{Drag}} \quad \frac{(L)}{(D)}$$

Although the side of the triangle adjacent to the angle in question is
not the same in each case, this doesn't matter with small angles, such
as typical values of glide angles.

To be of any practical use, the glide angle or ratio must be known
throughout the speed range of the glider. What the designer sets out
to achieve is subsequently confirmed by actual measurements and

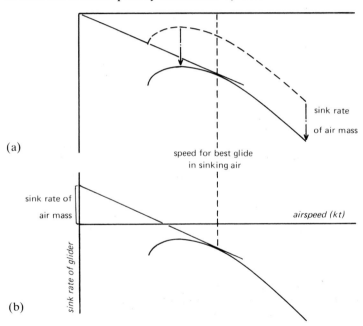

Figure 48. *The polar: best glide in sinking air.*
Basic polar and best glide angle.
(a)   For sinking air the polar is considered to be moved down the axes an
       amount equal to the rate at which the air is sinking. More conve-
       niently, the rate at which the air is sinking can be marked off the
       vertical axis and the tangent drawn from that point, as in (b).
(b)   Whichever of the two is done, the answer is the same. This is the
       method that was used to determine the speed of 69 kt in the earlier
       example (see page 134).

the information presented to the pilot, initially in the form of a graph, an example of which is shown in Figure 47.

The slope of the line (the tangent) represents the best, i.e. shallowest, angle which can be related to the polar; any other line would slope more steeply, and moreover cut the polar in two places.

Once this principle is accepted, this process of drawing a tangent and determining the airspeed of the point of contact can be used to determine the right speed to fly, taking into account the wind, sinking air and, less obviously, the rate of climb. The concept of doing this is shown in Figure 48.

The same principle applies when taking into account the wind, but in this case the polar is moved sideways or, more conveniently, the tangent is drawn from a point appropriate to the wind speed, as shown in Figure 49:

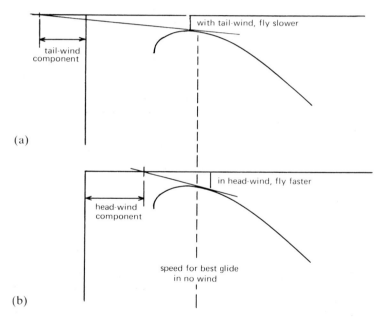

Figure 49. The best speed to fly, allowing for wind.
(a)   For a tail-wind component the wind strength is taken to the left of the vertical axis; the appropriate speed will be less than the 'best glide speed'.
(b)   For a head-wind the allowance is made by drawing the tangent from a point to the right of the vertical axis.

This last information would be used for a glide calculator; all the previous explanation, for a speed-to-fly ring. The latter, incidentally, was originally devised by the American Dr Paul MacCready.

It only remains to introduce one further concept or principle regarding the polar and speed-to-fly, and this relates to going as *fast* as possible rather than as *far* as possible. All that has gone before in this chapter relates to maximum distance.

When lift is strong it should be evident that the glider can be flown more quickly between the thermals than when the lift is weak. The mathematical proof of this point and the previous ones is beyond the scope of this book.* If you can accept the principle, practical experience will bear out the theory. The interesting point in determining the speed to fly in relation to the climb rate is that the use of the polar and the tangents is the same as that for sinking air. From the diagram, Figure 50, some new facts can be drawn.

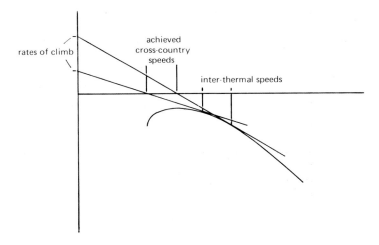

Figure 50. Flying speed / achieved cross-country speed relationship.
Where the tangent for a particular climb rate cuts the horizontal axis, the speed given is the achieved cross-country speed. It is worth noting that flying faster (because the lift is stronger) does not make too much difference to cross-country speed. The whole of this theory is based on the assumption that the next thermal will be as strong as the last one, and one cannot always rely on that.

---

* For the mathematically minded, *New Soaring Pilot* (Third Edition) is recommended; see Bibliography.

The principles of MacCready speed-to-fly-ring derivation are given in more detail in Appendix 1. However, the concepts for flying for speed should be considered in the light of the following.

Why fly MacCready?*

Many cross-country pilots accept as a tenet of faith that the speed to fly between thermals is that indicated by the MacCready ring when this is set to the average achieved rate of climb. If this rate is accurately known, then there is no doubt that it is the optimum setting for maximum cross-country speed.

But there are other important factors to be considered: the probability of completing the task, and the work-load on the pilot. The maximum probability occurs when the glider is flown between thermals at maximum L/D, that is with the MacCready ring set at zero. At slower or faster speeds the chance of completion decreases rapidly. This can be calculated mathematically† with a probability of zero meaning certain failure and one certain success. Mathematical calculations are only as truthful as the completeness of the factors included and the assumptions made, and in the complex field of gliding the full story is never told. But the results shed light on what is happening and afford genuine insights which can be applied in practice. The following figures were calculated for the Kestrel 19; although the values will be different for other gliders, the same principles apply and the same lessons are to be learnt.

Assume the task is a 300-km triangle, the day giving thermals 6 km apart enabling an average rate of climb of 3 kt to be consistently achieved within the operating height band of say 2,500 feet, with little or no wind. The results of flying in these conditions at an inter-thermal speed for minimum sink and also for MacCready speed settings from zero (best L/D) to 5 kt are shown opposite.

The implications are clear. The chances of getting around the task are by far the best with the MacCready ring set at zero (best L/D), and this is indicated when speed is not important and there is time in hand. Less height will need to be climbed, fewer thermals to be found and exploited, the work-load will be much less and the flight less tiring. If cross-country speed is the criterion then the inter-

* 'Why Fly MacCready?' by Paul Thompson was first published in *Lasham and Gliding* magazine.

† 'A Stochastic Cross-country' by Anthony Edwards, *Sailplane and Gliding* magazine, February, 1963.

	Min sink	MacCready ring setting					
		0	1	2	3	4	5
Interthermal speed (Kts)	40	53	64	73	80	87	92
Height climbed (ft × 1000)	23·6	19·8	20·8	23·7	26·6	30·0	33·7
No. of thermals used	10	8	9	10	11	12	14
Cross-country speed (km/h)	54·5	69·7	78·2	81·5	82·3	81·7	79·5
Time taken	5h30m	4h18m	3h50m	3h41m	3h39m	3h40m	3h46m
Probability of completion	0·66	0·83	0·79	0·66	0·51	0·36	0·22

thermal speed should be that indicated when the ring is set at the average rate of climb actually achieved; the extra speed however is gained only by increasing the risk of landing out or falling into a time-consuming hole. Perhaps a compromise would be the best solution, such as setting the MacCready ring to say one-third of the best rate of climb consistently indicated on the vario, or maybe two-thirds of the realistically estimated average rate of climb.

Of course these figures ignore dolphining (which can increase cross-country speed dramatically), the vagaries of the weather which makes fools of the best of us, and the 'miracle ingredient' that some pundits seem to have. But it may be that most of us have been flying too fast, without giving too much thought to the probabilities we're playing with. The figures tell us something. Think on it!

If the foregoing raises some doubts in your mind then you should consider the purpose of your flight(s). It might be argued that all badge-qualifying flights are distance tasks rather than speed; speed or lack of it is only significant if the soaring day is not long enough to complete the task.

The final consideration regarding speeds-to-fly is in relation to the height band being used on a particular flight. If the lift really is strong, then it may well be desirable to speed up, especially if the earlier part of the flight was slow. It is worth noting that one's subjective impression of climb rate is rarely anything like the actual figure, bearing in mind that the rate is based on the total time in the thermal, which includes centring time. Four knots indicated may well mean only two knots average.

Let us suppose that there are 6-kt thermals about and that, being conservative, the speed-to-fly ring has been set to 3 kt (by rotating the arrow from zero to 3 kt up). Going confidently and remaining high will justify maintaining that setting, but as you get lower the ring should be progressively 'wound back' to zero; certainly below 2,000 feet, staying airborne is the name of the game.

Glide calculations

It was suggested in an earlier chapter that the use of a local-soaring calculator was a useful aid to judgement. With improvements in glider performance it becomes impossible to judge or 'guesstimate' a final glide. To give you some idea of the problem involved, a glider with a best glide angle of 1 in 35 would cover 28 nm from 5,000 ft e.g. the entire third leg of the sample cross-country, pages 99–115. With a 15-kt tail-wind, the distance becomes 39 nm from 5,000 feet – it makes the mind boggle. In practice, very few pilots would set out to glide such a distance at the speed for best glide angle, preferring to be nearer and fly faster before final gliding. The variables in the equation are the distance to go, the speed to fly and the height necessary. A simple example will illustrate the point: see Figure 51.

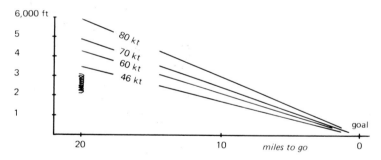

Figure 51. The choice of height-to-climb / glide-speed for final glide.
The glider (1:35 glide ratio) is at 2,000 feet in a 4-kt thermal, 20 nm from its goal; there is no wind. The pilot has to decide the height to which he will climb and the speed at which he will final-glide. The choices, among others, are:
(a)   Climb to 3,500 ft and glide at 46 kt.
(b)   Climb to 4,200 ft and glide at 60 kt.
(c)   Climb to 4,800 ft and glide at 70 kt.
(d)   Climb to 5,900 ft and glide at 80 kt.

The figures to be reconciled are the extra time taken climbing against the quicker glide. From the initial 2,000 ft, the figures are:

	Time to climb	Time to glide	Total
(a)	3·75 min.	26	29·75
(b)	5·5	20	25·5
(c)	7·0	17·1	24·1
(d)	9·75	15·0	24·75

The answer is (c). If the computer is examined it can be seen at the top that there is a scale of speed-to-fly against rate of climb, and that 70 kt is the recommended speed for a 4 kt thermal and a glide with 1:35 glide ratio.

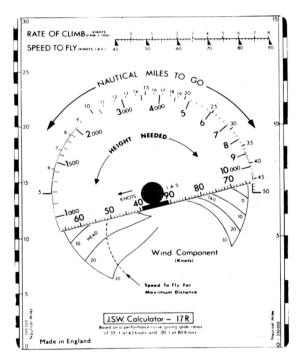

Figure 52. The final-glide calculator.
The calculator is set with the 70 kt speed value cutting the zero wind component on the right hand side. Against 20 on the nautical miles to go scale, read 4,800 ft.

A situation that might arise in practice is that if the thermal petered out at, say, four thousand feet and it was thought unlikely that further lift would be found then the calculator could be used to determine the speed to fly. See Figure 53.

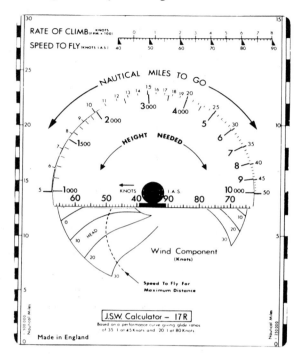

Figure 53. Using the glide calculator to determine the speed to fly.
By setting 4,000 ft against 20 nm the speed to fly can be read off where the zero wind line intersects the speed scale; the answer is 57 kt.

Another facility that this type of computer offers is to give the speed to fly for maximum distance. This is shown in Figure 54.

Finally there is one other piece of information which can be determined from the calculator, and that is the strength of the thermal needed to make progress against the wind. Using the rate of climb against speed-to-fly scale at the top of the calculator (for the previous example of a 10-kt head-wind) then the minimum strength of lift that will enable the pilot to make progress against the wind is 0·7 kt, this figure being taken from the upper scale against the speed determined in the previous example (50 kt). This means that a climb rate of 0·7 kt would in fact only enable the pilot to maintain his

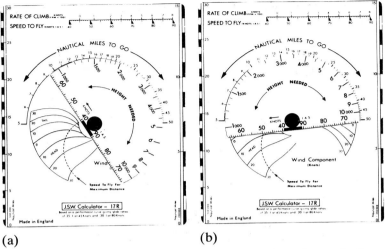

(a)   (b)

Figure 54. Using the glide calculator to determine distance that can be flown (allowing for wind).

At (a) the broken line can be seen; to determine the maximum distance that can be flown for a given wind component rotate the centre part of the calculator so that its lower edge passes through the intersection of the speed-to-fly-for-maximum-distance line and the appropriate wind line. At (b) this is determined for a 10-kt head-wind and the appropriate speed to fly is 50 kt.

© 1972		TAIL						HEAD					
↓	↑	25	20	15	10	5	−	5	10	15	20	25
1·40	−	52	48	45	41	38	34	31	27	24	20	16
1·55	1	49	46	43	40	37	33	30	27	24	21	17
2·08	2	41	39	36	34	32	29	27	24	22	20	17
2·66	3	35	33	32	30	28	26	24	22	20	18	16
3·30	4	31	29	28	26	24	23	21	20	18	17	15
3·82	5	28	26	25	24	22	21	20	19	17	16	15
4·28	6.	26	25	23	22	21	20	19	17	16	15	14

Figure 55. The Australian WAC computer. (a) on the back of the calculator is a table of glide angles based on MacCready ring settings – the figures 1–6 down the left-hand side and the wind components – tail-winds in the table on the left and head-winds on the right. The example indicated is for a 2-kt climb rate and a 10-kt head-wind; reading across and down from these two values gives a figure of 24 which is the glide gradient. (The figures in the boxes of thicker black lines have a margin for error of 15%.)

position rather than make progress against the wind. It would not mean that he would reject lift of that strength if the alternative were a field landing.

Computers or calculators come in many different forms. The simple one – the JSW – must be used in conjunction with a map; others of slightly more advanced design incorporate the map. The two sides of such a calculator are shown in Figures 55 (a) and (b).

It should be noted that this particular computer of Australian origin, the WAC, is designed for use with a one-million map; if used

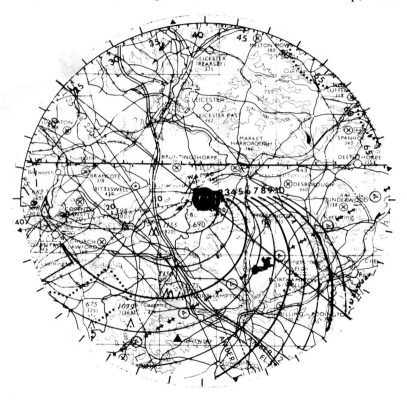

Figure 55. (b) On the front, the cursor, the rotatable arm, is set against the gradient value of 24 and its opposite end (by rotating the whole top transparent disc) over the glider's position on the map. The curved lines where they intersect the line of the cursor either give the height to climb to in the last thermal, or are used to monitor the progress of the final glide.

with a half-million map the 10,000 ft line corresponds to 5,000 ft. The appropriate speeds to fly are of course given by the speed-to-fly ring, and are not presented on the computer itself.

Glide calculators, whatever form they may take, are an essential part of cross-country soaring at an early stage of experience, to show when or whether the task can be completed and later to assist in completing the final stage of the flight as quickly as possible. Practice with such calculators is essential and every opportunity should be taken to improve ability in using them.

7 Problems and Remedies

Soaring started by using the wind where it was deflected upwards by ridges, and so the early gliding sites were situated on hill tops. This is where you will find the majority of long-established clubs. Present-day soaring is predominantly in thermals, with an increasing use of 'wave lift' as knowledge and spread of expertise in this aspect of the sport increases.

However, even with increased awareness and skill in other forms of soaring, if there is a ridge it is inevitable and natural that a pilot will use it as a means of staying airborne – if it's the only way, why not? Use of the hill lift may, and often does, result in a pilot failing to develop the skills necessary for thermal soaring, and in this respect the hill constitutes a definite handicap to progress. To typify the hillsite pilot, the term 'hill-bound' is used and it is the purpose of this chapter to help a pilot recognise this state and perhaps overcome it.

The basics of ridge soaring
Given a steady wind not disturbed by thermal or wave activity, there will be a definite limit to the height that can be achieved in the hill lift; this will be directly related to the height, slope and contour of the hill and the strength of the wind. The hill lift will be better in some areas than in others, perhaps where the wind is exactly at right angles to the slope or there is some funnelling effect such as a gully or 'bowl'. This stronger lift may be exploited by S-turning to gain slightly more height than would be achieved by simply beating along the length of the ridge, but this extra height will probably be to little or nor avail. (If there is wave lift, it may help the pilot to contact it.) The only consideration in using lift in this way is that of airmanship. Can it be done without significant conflict with other traffic? The S-turn complies with the basic hill-soaring rules but would be

regarded as bad airmanship if it conflicted with other ridge traffic. The principle of 'S' turning in areas of better lift is of more consequence when the hill lift is mixed with thermals. A ridge facing the sun is a good source of thermals for the simple reason that the ground near the base of the ridge will be at right angles to the sun's rays and therefore absorb more heat. In the hill-and-thermal lift mix, there will be areas where one reinforces the other and areas where sinking air between thermals cancels out the ridge lift. Exploitation of the thermal by S-turning will enable the pilot to climb much higher than he would by simply beating up and down the ridge. Once the glider is well above the rest of the ridge traffic and well above the top of the hill (or ridge) then it may be flown in the conventional thermal-soaring way.

In practice, it is remarkable how high one can get solely by S-turning; the characteristics of the thermal from a ridge are a distortion which lends itself to this technique. The opportunity to get 'up and away' is frequently shown to the hillside pilot by visitors from flat sites who are much more thermal-soaring orientated. Although this more aggressive or positive style of flying is not an end in itself, it must be recognised as a first step to greater freedom and a lessening dependence on ridges.

If this dependence was the only factor in making a pilot 'hill-bound', then it might not be too difficult to develop an attitude more orientated to cross-country flying, but the site itself imposes other limitations.

The typical (United Kingdom) hill site will be from five hundred to fifteen hundred feet above sea level; in other words take-off height is already that much nearer to cloud base. The consequence is that even when a pilot has climbed to cloud base his height above site will probably not seem adequate to set off across country, despite the fact that a few miles downwind the height above ground increases considerably. Another factor is the tendency for the cloud to build up over the high ground, cutting off the sun's rays and spoiling the convection in at least the local area. It is not at all unusual for the cloud base to be lower over this high ground and these features together would make all but the most intrepid cross-country pilots reluctant to set off.

The overall situation has a detrimental effect on the environment for the up-and-coming pilot who, seeing no more purpose to gliding than soaring a ridge with an occasional flight in thermals or wave lift, is unlikely to aspire – let alone attempt – to be a cross-country pilot. The statistic which would be most enlightening in this context is the number of pilots who, having got their Silver 'C', ever go across country again. For hillsite pilots, I suspect the answer would be very few.

If you are hill-site trained and have ambition to become a cross-country pilot, then the remedy lies in your own hands. You must either break down the psychological barriers yourself or move to another site – temporarily at least – where the environment, in the attitude of the other pilots, and the conditions are more conducive to cross-country soaring.

In this context it may well be appropriate to look at some of the ways in which pilots, whatever their proficiency, may be helped towards a broader experience and a greater fulfilment from the sport.

If asked to state aims for gliding as a sport there would be two, perhaps three, simple dictates:

1.   That the sport should offer the opportunity for the invidivual to get the maximum fulfilment appropriate to his ability.
2.   That pilots should enjoy the sport in the highest degree of safety possible.
3.   That those responsible for pilot training and supervision should remember that everyone is there to enjoy themselves.

In stating these aims, it must be recognised that not everyone wants the same thing from their gliding club; the variations are considerable. Some people settle for building winches, others for driving tractors or digging ditches; there is something for everyone to do. In terms of gliding progress too, it is up to the individual to decide what he wants. If the height of his ambition is to go solo and then tell stories about his gliding experience in the local pub then all well and good. Beyond this level, it is sometimes difficult to determine whether a pilot has achieved his ambition or has reconciled himself to his failures. I suspect, for instance, that there are many pilots who aspire to complete a 300-kilometre task, but who do not make any serious attempt because they believe themselves incapable of it, or feel they will lose face if they fail in the attempt. The aim therefore should be to help more pilots to achieve their secret ambitions by having a club environment conducive to trying.

One of the more stultifying and discouraging factors in this direction is the attitude of instructors. Shaw's adage, 'Those who can do, those who can't teach', often seems appropriate to gliding instruction. A particular channel along which a glider pilot can progress is that of becoming an instructor. Nowadays the experience of pilots before they qualify (as instructors) has increased considerably from their counterparts of ten or more years ago; Gold 'C's are not unusual, and the majority of new instructors will have cross-country experience beyond Silver 'C'. Becoming an instructor, however, may preclude much further progress as a solo and cross-country pilot. This builds problems for an instructor in a cross-country environment, for, in terms of teaching anything, there is no substitute for recent practice.

For anyone – pilot or instructor – there comes a time in his gliding experience when he needs help to progress beyond the point he has already reached if he is continue enjoyment of the sport. It is the ways in which this help can be given – it may not come unless it is asked for – that is of consequence. There are three basic ways in which help can be given; cross-countries in two-seaters, escorted cross-countries or a suitable cross-country-oriented environment, such as a task-week or competition.

Two-seater cross-countries
Two-seater cross-countries are rarely a part of the club's training programme for the simple reason that there is great demand for two-seaters for *ab initio* work; any suggestion that it should go cross-country will usually be rejected outright. The club's training philosophy has to be thoroughly re-thought if any change is to be brought about. Changes are taking place, however, if only to the extent of allowing club seaters to be used in task-weeks.

The effectiveness of the exercise has to be viewed in the light of the student's soaring ability, and psychological problems with regard to cross-country flying, as well as the glider to be used.

The glider
Developments and improvements in the performance of two-seaters in the last ten years have increased (especially compared with single-seaters) after a period of stagnation. The range of performance now extends from the conventional club two-seater to better than 40 : 1 glide performance. Inevitably there have been some compromises from the customer's point of view; cost, weight,

and to some extent complexity. The situation is complicated by the varying requirements of a gliding movement. Unless the club using a high-performance glider is a very large one, it may have to double for basic as well as advanced training. All the development and training philosophy factors may not be relevant to you however and either you have a chance to go across country in a two-seater or you have not. If you have, and you take the chance, then the way in which the flight will be conducted will depend on your instructor; he can either show you how to do it, or have you do all the flying and 'troubleshoot' your technique. The compromise is obviously to share the flying, and since the exercise may be a complicated one with elements of thermalling technique, sky reading, navigation and perhaps field landing, it may be necessary for the instructor to do quite a lot of the flying.

The eventual decision as to 'who does how much of what' may well leave you either with a sense of dissatisfaction, frustration, or worst of all, boggling at the ability of your instructor. He is faced with many decisions to give of his best, what is certain is that he will be striving to give you maximum benefit from the flight unless he is on some kind of 'ego trip'.

The chance of a two-seater cross-country should be taken if the opportunity arises (even an instructor will learn something about instructing technique, if not about cross-country flying).

Escorted cross-countries

Escorted cross-countries are the province of the specialist – or so it would seem. The method of working is to form up in the local area as soon after launch as possible and to facilitate this, radio – in the tug as well as the gliders – may be used. Once the group is together, the leader will set off with the other pilots flying in line astern.

There are obvious organisational difficulties such as getting a group of pilots with similar abilities, and there are practical problems if the group gets split – even if the separation is only vertical.

Since this book is largely concerned with ways in which you can help yourself it would constitute a digression to go into too much detail regarding this type of cross-country training. Suffice it to say that the method is of proven, indeed outstanding, effectiveness, and if you have ambitions which are ahead of your confidence then this sort of training may well be for you.* The final way to improve your cross-country performance is to attempt a 'task week'.

Task weeks

Unless you have been on a task week you will probably regard it as a competition and, while this may be true up to a point, you will find considerably less emphasis on the competitive spirit. The range of tasks set will take into account the pilot's shortcomings and his experience, with a view to gradual progress within the limitations of his confidence. Some of the 'firsts' on task weeks of which I have had first-hand experience have been:

1. Into-wind cross-countries of almost fifty kilometres by pilots without Silver 'C'.
2. Completion of a closed-circuit task.
3. Satisfactory field landings on failed closed-circuit tasks.

All of which have represented a considerable step-forward for the individual concerned and have given an impetus – as increased motivation – through an improving confidence and a recognition that the particular goal set is perhaps, after all, not an impossible one.

'Advanced training' is here to stay but as yet is in its infancy. Like all changes, it is slow to gather momentum; once it has, the demand for it will increase and its benefits will have far-reaching effects on gliding as a whole, with individuals gaining more fulfilment from the sport and a broader experience sooner.

* The only regular sources of this type of training (in the United Kingdom) are at the major gliding clubs and, to a lesser extent, through the BGA's Coaching Scheme.

8 Ground Crew Organisation, Flight Documentation, and Retrieving

One of the most notable changes in gliding in the last twenty years or so has been the reduction of out-landings, for the single reason that the majority of cross-country tasks are closed-circuit, and most of them successful at that. Even when the glider does land out, it may be retrieved by aerotow. Conventional road retrieving thus becomes less and less a part of gliding.

In many respects this is sad because there is a tremendous amount of fun to be had; the epic retrieves often make better stories then the flights themselves. Some are well worth recounting . . .

The flight was free-distance from North Hill in Devon in a Caproni Calif, and the wind stood fair for France. Although we made good time down to the Dover area, getting high enough for the crossing proved difficult. Having set course for France, it became evident that the best we could do was land a mile or two inland and so we turned back to England – sinking ignominiously to the ground at Lyminge, just north of Folkestone.

Here the real story starts; the field was a good one – big enough to aerotow out of – and as there was a gliding club a few miles away we took a taxi there to arrange for a tug. A club pilot went with the tug and the owner of the glider to the field and pulled the glider out. However, because of a lack of speed control on the tug pilot's part, the glider pilot could not keep station and had to release and land in a smaller field – too small to aerotow out of. The tug pilot returned to the first field; after a little while during which time both pilots contemplated their errors, they both went to the other's field – one by air and the other by hitching a lift. Needless to say the attempted aerotow retrieve had to be abandoned.

The retrieve crew back in Devon were now alerted (it was

1800 hr; the flight had ended at 1430 hr), and, after a fumble with cars because the electrics of the team car would not make the trailer's lights work, they duly set off. Fortunately, there was a spare car and keys for it. The two-girl crew arrived at Lasham about 2130 hr and persuaded two chaps to assist with the retrieve (the glider pilots at this point had had dinner and were on the point of going to bed). The four-person crew arrived at the field at 0200 hr only to find that the gate was locked. They decided quite rightly that they would not disturb the farmer but they did advise the glider pilots of progress so far. The next snag was that the supernumerary crew had to be back to Lasham by 0800 hr to go to work. They were duly taken there, the trailer being left behind. The original crew, now having driven four hundred miles and feeling slightly jaded, had breakfast and set off for Kent again, arriving about 1300 hr. By 1430 hr – 24 hours after the landing – the glider was in the trailer and we now had a choice of two cars to tow back with. We stopped at Lasham on the way back to Devon to have a bite to eat and a drink. The pilot had now taken control of the retrieve and being a perspicacious fellow, recognised the imminent failure of the crew's sense of humour. They were put into the back of the car with an enormous pile of sandwiches and three bottles of wine; the crisis was averted. The retrieve was completed by 2030 hr; the total time on the road was twenty-six and a half hours, and we had covered eight hundred miles; it's probably not a record, but it was extremely memorable, and in retrospect a lot of fun.

This does however show that retrieves made on an ad hoc basis can be less than efficient. Other stories – some of them legend – all serve to show that some organisation is essential to well co-ordinated retrieves. A certain amount of organisation is essential to the flight itself, and since this chapter is essentially about management, of the glider, pilot, flight, trailer, retrieve vehicle, and crew, all these will be dealt with here.

The whole scheme of things relates to the flight being planned; even if it is a closed-circuit task there may still be the need for a retrieve, and this should always be assumed. The better organised flights will start with preparation the evening before, and all the kit that can be put together should be. Kit will include all the equipment ancillary to glider, pilot and trailer.

Navigational equipment: the 'Nav-Bag'

Navigational equipment is very much a matter of personal preference but the minimum requirements are:

1. All relevant maps, up-to-date with latest controlled airspace information.
2. Pencils or Chinagraph marker, and a means of sharpening them.
3. Scale rules (in the appropriate units – probably kilometres); it is nonsense to make a mistake in converting kilometres to statute miles or nautical miles. If you don't have a scale rule in kilometres, have a conversion table handy.
4. Protractor.
5. Glide calculator.
6. Camera and films for turning-point photography.

The best practice is to keep all the equipment in a bag or case designed for the purpose.

The glider: ancillary equipment

This includes all the detachable items which may need preparation before hand:

1. Barograph. It should be wound up, the paper or foil fitted to the drum and smoked if necessary. Do not put a base line on it if preparing it the night before the flight – the pressure may change. Provision for sealing it should be available.
2. Glider batteries. These should be charged the night before.
3. Parachute (pilot's and tail).
4. Ballast weights, if required.
5. Water-ballasting equipment. Containers, and any tubes, pipes, funnels or connectors essential to filling the wing tanks should be checked. (These are probably best kept with the trailer.)
6. Cameras, films, camera mounts, and sealing arrangements.
7. 'Tie-down' equipment in case the glider has to be left after landing out.
8. Any other miscellaneous items.

The pilot

Personal equipment for the flight will depend on the climate and the weather, and should anticipate the range of possible changes.

1. Clothing to suit the conditions, including an extra sweater, waterproofs and (if flying in shorts) trousers.
2. Head-gear: sun hat and sun glasses.
3. Shoes suitable for walking – sandals are often not adequate.
4. Money, including change for the telephone, and/or a telephone credit card as well as as any relevant telephone numbers.

The car and trailer
Ideally, the trailer should be hitched to the car; this minimises the risk of bringing the wrong trailer and the amusing-in-retrospect experience of a trailer taken to the retrieve site with a glider already in it. Requirements are:

1. Trailer attached to the car with lights checked, number plates correct, and fittings stowed.
2. Keys to the car and the trailer should be readily available.
3. The driver (crew chief) should be briefed on the phoning-in and landing-report procedures, and ideally know the general direction of the flight (a last minute change of mind on the direction for free-distance flight has more than once resulted in glider and retrieve going in opposite directions).
4. Maps in the car to facilitate the retrieve.
5. The driver should be briefed if there are any critical speeds for the car–trailer combination or any unusual characteristics or handling features.

Flight Documentation

The barograph
A barograph must be carried for all badge-claim flights, and should have been inspected and sealed by the official observer before the flight. It must be presented to an observer (not necessarily the same one) with the seal unbroken after the flight. The observer should know that the barograph was carried on the flight in question; the barograph trace must be marked up with:

1. Pilot's name.
2. Date of flight.
3. A base line.
4. Barograph make and serial number.

5.   The official observer's signature and number (it may be helpful to print his name as well).

Flight declarations*

Declarations by the pilot of departure point, turning point(s) and
goal shall be written on a single sheet or board and include the date,
the time, the identifying number of the glider and the signature of
the pilot and official observer. For a flight with turning point using
photographic evidence, the declaration shall appear on the film
immediately preceding the photograph(s) of the turning point(s).

Evidence of point of release

There will be a limit to launch height for Silver 'C' distance flights†
and it may also be the case that a dropping zone some distance away
from the home airfield is necessary (if for example going to another
airfield marginally 50 km away, or even slightly less).

For closed-circuit badge tasks the glider should not be released
along track but either overhead at the airfield at which the flight is
commenced or to the opposite side of the initial track.

The barograph should show a low point following release in order
to determine the starting altitude. Although a tug pilot's evidence is
accepted, this low point is particularly important for height claims.

Photographic evidence (from *FAI Sporting Code*)

The requirements for photographing turning points are dealt with
elsewhere (see Appendix 3). The sequence of photographs should
be on a single uncut length of film. It is imperative that normal
commercial sources of film processing are briefed on this point – in
fact it may be better not to trust a film to other than someone in
gliding. The photographs should prove that they were taken:

1.   By the pilot of the glider on the flight in question. The photograph should include a picture of the declaration – either the
task board or the hand-written declaration – so long as it
includes the information given in flight declaration.

---

* *FAI Sporting Code* Section 3, Class D, Gliders, 1981.
† The height between the point of release and the point of landing shall not
exceed more than 1% of distance covered; for a flight of 50 km, 1% =
500 metres = 1,640 ft.

2. Of the declared turning points from the correct location and in the correct sequence.

3. Between the time of last crossing of the start line and crossing of the finishing line.

This last point (3) is not generally relevant to badge flights. It should be noted that a new film must be used for each flight.

Photographic control

The camera should be loaded with an unused film and sealed by an official observer who should take, or observe the pilot take, a photograph of the Declaration board before take-off. The camera, or the observer's seal, must be marked with the identifying number of the glider.

Following landing an official observer will take charge of the sealed camera and have the film developed and kept uncut.

Landing reports

Landing reports are required for badge claims and the appropriate section of the badge-claim form can be used. The report should be signed by one official observer or two other witnesses, who must give their addresses; it should contain a landing position given as exactly as possible and the time of landing.

Completion of the claim

This is the responsibility of an official observer, but his lot and yours is made easier if all the documentation is in order. The list of checks below should follow the glider's daily inspection, with certain items (asterisked) being double-checked prior to take-off:

Check list

    Check of NOTAMs.*
    Flight declaration made.
    A photograph of declaration board taken.
    Barograph: 1. Base line.
             2. Wound-up and on correct rotation rate.
             3. Sealed.
             4. Switched on and correctly stowed.

* 'Notices to Airmen'; see Appendix 2.

Camera(s). Two are recommended to guard against the risk of a malfunction. They should be correctly fitted to the mounts, or easily accessible if they are to be hand-held.

Maps, accessible and marked up as required.

Any in-flight facilities: food, drink, 'plumbing', sun hat, sunglasses, all readily accessible.

Retrieving

The landing report

The landing report relayed to the crew either by radio or by telephone will ideally have a contact telephone number – usually the farmer's – in case of difficulty in linking up. Remember that this may be done in the dark. A typical landing report form for posting on the club's out-landings board is shown below:

Pilot's
name _____

Glider name
or number _____

Full postal address
of landing place _____

_____

_____

Tel No _____

Taken by _____ time _____

Day of
week/date _____

Any other
Information _____

Please write clearly, and then clip on Retrieve Board.

The crew

A one-man crew may be sufficient to retrieve the modern single-seater, especially if there are rigging aids. It may be better to have two crew members if there is some navigating to be done and a risk of having to reverse a trailer – never an easy task alone.

Joining up

The last mile or two to the glider is often the most difficult part of the retrieve, and this is where detailed instructions from the pilot regarding access are valuable, preferably combined with some initiative on his part to meet the trailer, provided there is only one route into the area in which the glider has landed. If radio is fitted this may assist with the link up but ground-to-ground range can be very limited in undulating country, and it makes the assumption that the pilot has stayed with the glider. This is sometimes not the case; the pilot may be enjoying someone's hospitality and regaling them with tales of his daring exploits. Retrieve crews do occasionally lose their sense of humour in such circumstances.

De-rigging the glider

More with club gliders than privately owned ones, there is a slight risk that due to someone's oversight no-one knows how to de-rig the glider. In this circumstance proceed with great care; a glider can easily be damaged by careless or hurried de-rigging. An essential part of pilot's training must include this basic skill.

Proper stowage of the parts in the trailer is also essential, and generally with a club glider it should be the responsibility of *one* member to see that trailer equipment is properly maintained.

The retrieve

There may be some pressure – the need to go to work in the morning, say – which encourages haste in completing the retrieve. Nowadays, the design of trailers is good in terms of stability and ease of towing. However there is often a limiting speed at which the car-trailer combination becomes unstable, and if you have limited experience of 'trailing' then it is not something to discover or experiment with at the end of a long and tiring day.

If a combination does become unstable the first requirement is to avoid over-controlling. The remedy may depend on several factors, such as whether you are going up- or down-hill, the wind, and any disturbing effect such as overtaking vehicles. The way of gaining control will generally be by reducing speed, but this should not be done in haste. Rapid speed reduction can cause 'jack-knifing', or eventual rolling of the trailer or even the car. Just occasionally the situation can be brought under control by accelerating but generally if the speed is high – which is usually the case when things go wrong – then there may not be sufficient power to do this.

Suffice it to say that with more than thirty feet of trailer behind the car, there is a strong case for caution and a responsible attitude to other road users. The art of good trailer driving is an essential one to a good image for gliding. In this context, the ability to reverse a trailer is something that needs practice – take the opportunity whenever you can.

Team spirit

There is possibly no more satisfying experience – other than having made the flight yourself – than carrying out a well-organised retrieve. It would be an ungrateful pilot indeed who didn't recognise this as perhaps the only true team-element of the sport. Giving credit for an efficient retrieve is all part of it. There are, unfortunately, a very few pilots who, even if the crew are waiting in the field for them, will always find something to complain about. If, of course, they have failed in a competition task, then they may want to take it out on someone. A good crew in this circumstance will keep silent (or behave in a way best suited to the psychological need of their pilot). But the fact remains that, however much the sport is a solo one, a team is still needed in the end. It is this as much as anything which makes the sport what it is – a combination of people, experiences, thrills and excitement.

Appendix 1

Principles of Flight
The following diagrams deal with the performances of a glider, and the use of that performance to best advantage.

1. This diagram reminds you that the glide angle is the ratio of the lift divided by the drag. The glide angle can be more usefully related to airspeed and sink rate.

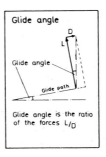

Glide angle

Glide angle is the ratio of the forces $L/_D$

2. This is shown here: the ratio of the forward speed divided by the sink rate is a measure of the glide angle.

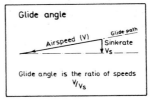

Glide angle

Glide angle is the ratio of speeds $V/_{Vs}$

3. Here the information from the previous two diagrams is combined which should make it easy to see that the ratios L/D and V/Vs, relating as they do to identical angles, are interchangeable. These ratios hold true for glide angles of better than 1 in 10. Now the glider's glide angle is variable with speed.

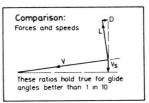

Comparison:
Forces and speeds

These ratios hold true for glide angles better than 1 in 10

4.   The different values are normally
      presented on this graph which is
      called a polar. It might at first
      sight appear to be an upside-
      down graph, but, logically, values
      of rate of sink are shown as
      increasing in a downward direc-
      tion.

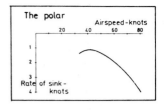

5.   Just consider two points from this
      graph: at an airspeed of 60 knots
      the sink rate is 2 knots so the glide
      angle is 60 divided by 2, i.e. 30.
      At 80 knots the sink rate is 4 and
      the glide angle equals 20. Where
      then on this graph does the best
      glide angle lie?

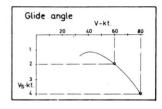

6.   In this diagram a tangent is drawn
      from the intersection of the axes
      (of the graph) to the polar, the
      point of contact between them –
      the tangent and the polar, that is –
      gives the speed for the best glide
      angle. This point is so important
      that it is stated again: the speed
      for best glide angle is determined
      by drawing a tangent from the
      origin of the axes (i.e. where air-
      speed and sink rate = 0) to the
      polar.

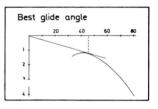

7.   The triangle originally considered
      looked like the upper diagram but
      there is no reason why it should
      not be drawn as in the lower dia-
      gram which makes it easier to
      relate to the tangent to the polar.
          The best glide angle is achieved
      when the angle is as small as it can
      be – best V/Vs ratio. (Bear in
      mind that because of the different

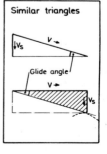

scales used on the vertical and horizontal axis, although the glide angle is numerically correct, the actual angle in the diagram is not.) One other point you might have picked up is that in the upper diagram airspeed is measured along the inclined side of the triangle whilst in the lower one it is measured along the horizontal side. Because the angles are actually so small this is of no account.

8. If we now look at the polar again it will be obvious that the triangle with the tangent forming one side is the same as in the previous diagram. Any triangle related to any other point on the polar will represent a steeper glide angle.

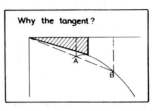

Why the tangent?

9. This is shown here together with the triangle for best glide angle. Note that the glide angles given by the points A and B are the same because the triangles to them are similar.

Now I want to show you that the best glide angle will be achieved at different speeds in various conditions. Consider the case of flying through air sinking at 4 knots.

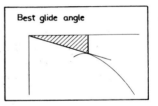

Best glide angle

10. If we fly at best glide angle, a speed of 46 knots for the particular glider – a Dart 17R – then, assuming it takes 30 seconds to cross with a total sink rate i.e. air-mass plus glider 4 + 1·2 = 5·2 knots, which is 520 f.p.m.; in ½ minute the height loss will be 260 ft.

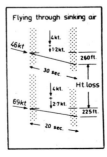

Flying through sinking air

Fly through this air at 69 knots, then the height loss is reduced to 225 ft. Not a big saving, you may say, but it is 15% and on a cross country if this height is wasted then it does mean extra time in thermals, or more thermals by comparison with a pilot flying at the right speed. How is the correct speed for the conditions determined?

11. This diagram shows you. For air sinking at 4 knots the tangent is drawn from a point 4 knots up the vertical axis and the answer that comes out is 69 knots. (Another way of achieving the same end is to move the whole of the polar 4 knots bodily downwards on the axes and draw the tangent from the zero point.) It should be noted that this calculation is concerned with having the glider fly the maximum possible distance. There are other considerations; namely:

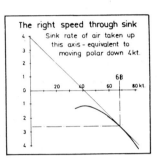

The right speed through sink

Sink rate of air taken up this axis - equivalent to moving polar down 4 kt.

12. Flying for speed. The speed flown between thermals depends on the achieved rate of climb in the thermal. The construction with the polar is the same as that used previously.

Flying for speed

The speed flown between thermals depends upon the achieved rate of climb in the thermal

The concept of flying for speed is relevant not only to competition flying but to large badge tasks when a certain speed must be maintained to complete the distance in the available hours of soaring.

13. In this diagram the rate of climb assumed is 2 knots. Note that this value is determined from an altimeter and a stop watch, not the variometer. The speed to fly is 57·5 knots, say 58. There is one other assumption – that the next thermal will be of the same strength.

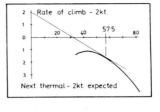

  Indeed this is the whole basis of the theory. If the rate of climb had been 4 knots then the construction would have been the same as that for flying through sinking air at 4 knots. as in diagram 11.

14. Taking into account two considerations – speed and distance would be dealt with as shown here. If the climb had been at 2 knots in the thermal then the speed to fly would be 58 knots. If then the glider was flown into air sinking at 2 knots then the appropriate speed would become 68 knots – which you will note is the same speed as flying through air sinking at 4 knots. The construction is the same for either consideration. To make sure you have got the idea here is another example.

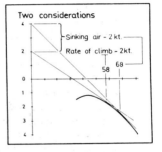

15. Determined in this case for either a climb rate of 6 knots, in which case the answer is 80 knots – flying for speed, or flying through air sinking at 6 knots and flying for distance.

  Now this information is best presented to the pilot in the form of a speed-to-fly ring which is fitted to the variometer.

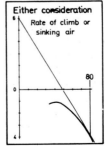

16. Here is such a speed-to-fly ring,
     named after the man who devised
     it. Notice an arrow against the
     variometer zero; the ring can be
     rotated but set in this position it is
     being used for distance. The
     speed at which the glider would
     be flown is 54 knots. A variome-
     ter reading of 3 knots down would
     suggest that the glider is in sinking
     air, or being flown fast, but we will
     assume the former.

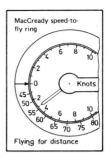

17. The ring is rotated when the
     glider is being flown for speed.
     Here the rate of climb has been 3
     knots. The variometer reading
     indicates that the speed to fly is
     67 knots. It should be evident that
     to arrive at all the information to
     complete a speed-to-fly ring then
     we would need to draw a lot of
     tangents from various points on
     the vertical axis. As several points
     have been considered they will be
     summarised.

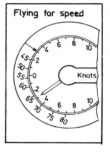

18. The graph isn't actually drawn
     here but the points previously
     determined are plotted. The
     point is placed where a horizontal
     line from the point on the vertical
     axis where the tangent is drawn
     intersects a vertical line from the
     point of contact of the tangent
     with the polar – join these points
     together to form the graph.

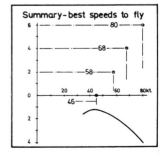

19. Here it is – the broken line. This new graph is used to determine the MacCready ring values. The values of speed on the ring were presented in 5 knot steps. This is neater than using 1 knot steps of climb rate and having speed steps with odd numbers, 46, 58, 69 etc.

In this case the example takes a speed of 65 knots and determines appropriate values of sink – a total of 5·6 knots i.e. 3·4 + 2·2.

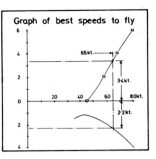

Graph of best speeds to fly

20. The variometer reading against which the speed is put is 5·6 knots and here is that single value on a speed-to-fly ring. If the variometer were reading 5·6 knots down then the speed should be 65 knots.

In the same way then the remaining values can be determined. Finally I want to show you how the ring would be used in practice.

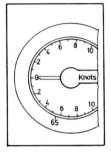

21. The state indicated here is the glider being flown at a speed of 46 knots (V) best glide angle: the variometer reads 1·2 knots (Vs) and the MacCready speed (VM) is 46 knots, so the glider is being flown correctly.

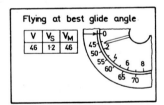

Flying at best glide angle

V	Vs	VM
46	1·2	46

22. It now flies into air sinking at 4 knots. The variometer now reads a total of 5·2 knots and indicates that the speed should be increased to 63 knots.

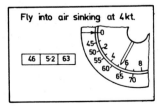

Fly into air sinking at 4kt.

46	5·2	63

23. However, if this is done the sink rate increases to 6·2 knots, the appropriate MacCready speed is 67 knots and a further speed increase is required.

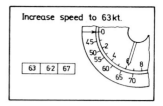

24. At 67 knots the variometer reading has increased to 6·5 knots and the MacCready speed is 68 knots.

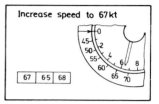

25. The situation is reached after a series of approximations where the actual and MacCready speeds are the same, assuming that is that the behaviour of the airmass has not altered.

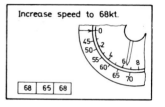

26. In practice, this is done much more easily by increasing the speed to a value a few knots above the MacCready value to achieve the recommended speed. Also in practice it is possible to anticipate the sink when leaving a thermal for example, so that the speed is increased before the sink is encountered.

In practice		V	V$_S$	V$_M$
Flying at best L/D		46	12	46
Into sinking air -4 kt.			52	63
Increase speed to 5kt above MacCready value		68	65	68

     To summarise, then, there are two uses for the speed-to-fly ring.

27. The first is flying for range when the arrow is set against zero on the variometer. The pilot will then fly at the speed indicated on the ring. This means that he is flying at the best speed through sinking air whenever it is encountered.

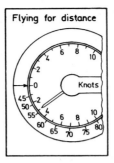

28. To fly for speed then, the arrow is set to the achieved rate to climb in the thermal. Remember that this is a timed rate of climb.

Evidently the better the rate of climb in a thermal the faster you should fly between thermals. The pilot will still adjust his speed to the value indicated by the ring and thus take into account the sinking air as well.

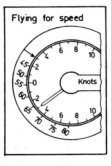

Appendix 2

British Gliding Association information sheet: Aeronautical Information and the Pilot's Responsibilities.

Introduction

Article 32 of the Air Navigation Order 1985 states that 'The commander of an aircraft registered in the United Kingdom shall satisfy himself before the aircraft takes off . . .' and 'that the flight can be safely made taking into account the latest information available as to the route and aerodromes to be used. . . .'

The key words are 'the latest information available'; it is the means of obtaining that information that this sheet is about.

The law

The legislation is laid out in two publications:

The Air Navigation Order 1985 (SI 1985 No. 1643);

The Rules of the Air and Air Traffic Control Regulations (SI 1985 No. 1714)

From time to time these Statutory Instruments (SIs) are amended by additional ones; the titles will be the same except for the addition of the words 'Amendment', 'Second Amendment', etc. Every two years or so, the Amendments will be incorporated and the Air Navigation Order 1980 will become the ANO 1985. The easy way to keep up-to-date with these Amendments is to purchase from the Civil Aviation Authority (CAA), *Air Navigation; the Order and Regulations* (CAP 393).This publication includes an up-dating service (if the appropriate fee is paid). It should not be necessary for a club or individual to have the SI publications unless concerned with interpretation of the law.

Generally, interpretation is done by the BGA where matters such as 'Flying for hire and reward' (tug pilots) or exemption from the

'Carriage by Air Act' (The 'blood-chit': see *Sailplane and Gliding* February–March 1978) are relevant to gliding operations.

Information for pilots
For all practical purposes the Aviation Legislation is presented to pilots in *United Kingdom Air Pilot* (CAP 32). This publication is available in three separate volumes or combined as one. *Volume 1* covers Air Traffic Rules and Services and is known as the RAC section. A subscriber to this publication (apart from the initial purchase price there is a subscription for the updating service) receives, from time to time, replacement pages incorporating changes. Changes will be necessary not only when the Order or the Rules are amended, but also when there are alterations to Controlled Airspace.

To be apprised of changes before they come into force, a pilot (or club) must subscribe to the NOTAM service (NOTAM means NOTice to AirMen).

NOTAMs
There are different classes of NOTAM, but only Class II would be available to a gliding club; Class I NOTAMs are transmitted by telex immediately via the Aeronautical Fixed Telecommunications Network, AFTN. Class II is divided into two categories:

Series 'A': these contain what amounts to immediate amendments to the UK Air Pilot (UKAP), and also details of new procedures or systems.
Series 'B': contain Temporary Navigational Warnings such as air displays, gliding competitions, weekend military low flying, parachuting etc., and are predominantly the ones which concern glider pilots. Since 1 April 1978, the Series 'B' NOTAMs have been available separately, making simpler the task of sorting out the relevant information.

There is one other type of NOTAM, that regarding a Royal flight. For Royal flights, existing or specially-classified, airspace is notified as 'purple'; that is, it is temporarily prohibited to other aircraft. The details of such flights are sent to all airfields including gliding clubs. If the airspace is notified at very short notice, then a telegram will be sent and, very occasionally, the details will be transmitted by telephone.

The only conceivable situation where a club did not receive these NOTAMs might be in the case of one which had recently formed or had changed sites; in either case it is necessary to write to the Aeronautical Information Service (AIS – see later for the address).

Navigational Warning Service

This service is provided by the regional Aeronautical Information Service (AIS) centres at Gatwick and Heathrow (Southern FIR), Manchester (Northern FIR) and Prestwick (Scottish FIR). The service, like NOTAMs, provides two categories of information:

1. A NOTAM record, i.e. a list of NOTAMs affecting the particular FIR.
2. A supplementary Navigational Warning which includes details of most temporary and permanent Navigational Warnings (usually parachuting and gliding are not listed unless restrictions to radio-equipped aircraft apply).

This service may be a suitable one to take unless the NOTAMs Service Service 'B' becomes available separately.

The final means by which Aeronautical Information is promulgated is:

Aeronautical Information Circulars

This service is a free one and gives details of new maps and charts, publications, changes to controlled airspace etc. There are two categories of AIC: 'white' containing the information already listed and 'pink' which concerns matters of safety – anything from R/T procedures and Emergency Services to skin contamination by aviation fuels and a Code of Practice (ref. 47/1977) for flight without radio.

Addresses

For NOTAMs and the United Kingdom Air Pilot (CAP 32):
Civil Aviation Authority,
Printing and Publications Service,
Greville House,
37 Gratton Road,
Cheltenham,
Gloucestershire GL50 2BN

For Aeronautical Information Circulars:
Aeronautical Information Service (AIS 2c),
Tolcarne Drive,
Pinner,
Middlesex, HA5 2DU

Publication prices
NOTAMs: annual subscription (includes initial set)
Series 'A' and 'B'	£16.75
Series 'A'	£ 9.25
Series 'B'	£ 7.50
NOTAMs: ring binder (holds both 'A' and 'B')	£ 8.00

In so far as these laws affect glider pilots, they are summarised in the
BGA publication *Laws and Rules for Glider Pilots*.

Appendix 3

Turning-point Photography

The majority of pilots make their first attempt at photographing a turning point when they already have a high work-load such as a 300-kilometre triangle or a competition task. Unless there are rules which actually specify that the camera must be mounted the chances

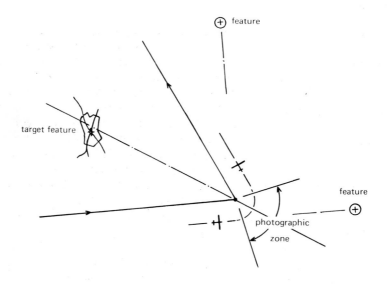

Figure A1. Turning-point photography.
(a)   A feature ahead to fly towards.
(b)   A feature which will be abeam (on the wing tip) as the turning point is passed.
(c)   A target feature to indicate the middle of the photographic zone.

are that it will be hand held. No wonder that turning-point pictures go wrong! A simple understanding of the principles involved, and a little practice, should lead to a much more organised approach and better results. The first thing to be convinced of is that a hand-held camera makes for poor results, and so a camera mount of some sort is essential. The position of the camera(s) should be such that the wing tip is in the picture, and allowance should be made for wing-tip deflection in positioning it. It will be possible, using a standard Instamatic, to achieve this with the camera pointing downwards at an angle of twenty degrees or so; it will also be useful if the camera is pointing slightly forwards as well.

The obvious aim in photographing a turning point is to fly the minimum distance possible past it and at the same time take the picture in the correct sector (see Figure 37). Orientation is of paramount importance; Figure A1 shows a way in which ground features can be used:

The turn required to photograph the turning point can be considered in two ways; either from getting around it in the shortest possible time, or giving oneself the best chance of taking a good picture. The one is a competition requirement; the other is more appropriate to a successful badge claim. Turning at a radius of two hundred feet (see Figure A2) from the turning point, at approximately sixty degrees of bank and at a speed of sixty knots, has the glider in the sector for only two and a half seconds or so, and makes the exercise into one demanding real precision. However, if looked at from the point of view of giving oneself more time in the sector and perhaps turning less steeply, then an immediate problem arises; with less bank the glider has to be flown much further beyond the turning point – approximately four times the distance – and even this amount would give less foreground to the picture.

For early attempts at this exercise it will generally be sufficient to fly past the turning point for a few seconds (60 kt is 100 ft per second), start a turn, and steepen it until the wing-tip is almost pointing at the t.p. Take the picture when the target feature is abeam, i.e. it is also on the wing-tip.

With the camera angled downwards 20° or so, using the wing-tip as a guide should guarantee the turning point being in the picture. The confidence that it is desirable to have before having to take an

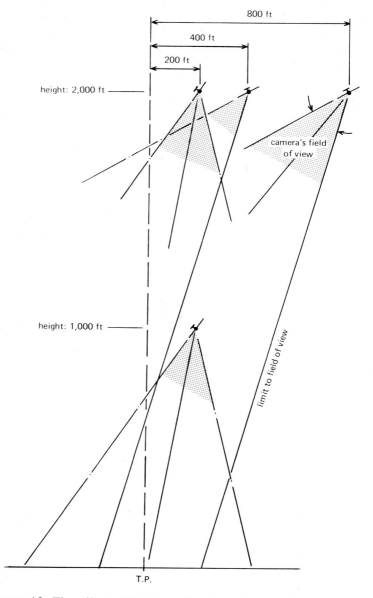

Figure A2. The effect of height and bank angle on radius required at turning-point.

important picture – usually for Gold 'C' distance/Diamond goal – comes from some practice beforehand; why not try it this winter!

To convince you of the bank angles and distance requirements, several alternatives are shown in Figure A2.

Appendix 4

Buying Your Own Glider
Whatever it is that prompts the thought, be it pride of ownership, dissatisfaction with the club's gliders, or frustration because there is not a glider available for cross-country flying, the possibility of buying your own glider or a share in one is likely to arise at some stage. The decision will, or should, be influenced by a number of factors, some of them interdependent. First of all we will assume that the decision to buy has been made in principle and look at it from the viewpoint of flying experience.

How much experience?
It is not unknown for a student under training – one who has not gone solo – to contemplate buying a share in a two-seater. There are certain advantages: you may be able to jump the queue for the club two-seater and you will probably fly with fewer instructors (those in the syndicate). Both are a definite advantage in a big club, where it may otherwise be difficult to fly with the same instructor often enough for him to know your standard and problems.

On the deficit side it is possible to fly with too few instructors, and not gain the broad outlook which would come only from flying with a number of instructors. If progress to solo is too rapid, then skill can outstrip airmanship – one needs exposure to a variety of weather conditions (different wind directions, strengths, turbulence, poor visibility etc.) to broaden experience.

The decision to join a syndicate prior to solo is not one that you are in a position to make alone; advice should be sought until quite a lot of experience has been gained.

After solo the decision will be made for much the same reasons as before, but a number of other factors become significant. Before considering, these however, the broad sub-division is whether you propose to buy a glider comparable with the single seaters in the club, or one which is much better. The factor which is relevant in this context is the particular glider's handling characteristics.

The glider's handling characteristics
For an inexperienced pilot, the requirement is for a glider with well-harmonised controls, one which is easy to fly accurately. (Experience, it should be noted, is not measured by launches and hours flown, but, amongst other things, by the number of types flown and the number of sites flown from.) The glider should also be vice-free; that is, not prone to spinning and with adequate warning of the impending stall.

It is possible to go into a lot more detail with factors such as the control loads (especially on the elevator, which should not be too light), the effectiveness of the airbrakes, and (perhaps of less significance but not always so) the seating position (upright/ reclining) and differences in cockpit layout and control complexity. All these factors must be considered in relation to the types of glider flown previously – too many differences in a single step may give rise to problems. Some of these problems are not always recognised. A glider which proves difficult to fly may preclude the pilot from ever becoming confident in his ability. Risks arise in this case when the work-load is high, for example in a field landing.

Confidence in one's glider is an essential ingredient for success. The choice is either a glider with similar performance and handling to those in the club fleet, or one which is significantly better in performance. The better-performance glider will often have much easier handling in terms of control harmonisation, but will have a much shallower approach angle, and demand more of the pilot's concentration in control of speed.

If the glider chosen is very different from anything flown previously, then the analogy of buying a bicycle which is too big for the child in question holds good. While the child grow into the bicycle, there are potential hazards. The root of the problem lies in the fact that most modern gliders demand to be flown accurately, and failure to do so results in approach and landing problems at the very least. If the glider demands too much of the pilot's concentration to fly it, this may be detrimental to concentration on other matters of equal or greater importance. The consequences are frights, incidents or even accidents.

One problem is that hard and fast rules cannot be made. Two pilots with similar experience might have differing aptitudes and better 'adaptability', and this might be dependent on their ages. The choice, therefore, needs careful consideration, and advice should certainly be sought.

Bibliography

Theory
Principles of Flight (Lecture notes). W. G. Scull. B.G.A. (1969).

Theory and Practice
New Soaring Pilot (3rd Rev. Ed.) A. Welch *et al.* John Murray (1977).
The Theory of Modern Cross-Country Gliding. F. W. Weinholtz (translated by D. Hope-Cross) New Zealand Gliding Kiwi.
Streckensegelflug. Helmut Reichmann. Motorbuch Verlag (1975). In English as *Soaring Cross Country* (Thompson Publications; Library of Congress Catalog Number 77-86598).
Ground Training for the Private Pilot Licence, Manual 2, 'Air Navigation & Aviation Meteorology'. R. D. Campbell (Aircraft Owners and Pilots Association).

Weather
Beginner's Guide to Weather Forecasting. S. Wells. Pelham Books (1975).
The Weather Guide. A. G. Forsdyke. Hamlyn (1969).
Meteorology for Glider Pilots (3rd International Edition). C. E. Wallington. John Murray (1977).

General
Laws and Rules for Glider Pilots. Edited by W. G. Scull. B.G.A.
Air Touring Flight Guide. Edited by R. Pooley. Airtour Associates (New edition annually).

Index